THE SELF?

The Self?

Edited by

Galen Strawson

Blackwell
Publishing

BLACKWELL PUBLISHING
350 Main Street, Malden, MA 02148-5020, USA
108 Cowley Road, Oxford OX4 1JF, UK
550 Swanston Street, Carlton, Victoria 3053, Australia

First published 2005 by Blackwell Publishing Ltd

First published in RATIO, an international Journal of analytic
philosophy, volume 17, No. 4.

Library of Congress Cataloging-in-Publication Data

ISBN 1-4051-2987-5

A catalogue record for this title is available from the British Library.

Set in 11 on 12 pt New Baskerville
by SNP Best-set Typesetter Ltd., Hong Kong
Printed and bound in the United Kingdom
by TJ International, Padstow Cornwall

The publisher's policy is to use permanent paper from mills that
operate a sustainable forestry policy, and which has been
manufactured from pulp processed using acid-free and elementary
chlorine-free practices. Furthermore, the publisher ensures that the
text paper and cover board used have met acceptable environmental
accreditation standards.

For further information on
Blackwell Publishing, visit our website:
www.blackwellpublishing.com

CONTENTS

INTRODUCTION

It is very natural for us to think that there is such a thing as the 'self' – an inner subject of experience, a mental presence or locus of consciousness that is not the same thing as the human being considered as a whole. The sense of the self arises almost irresistibly from fundamental features of human experience and is no sense a product of 'Western' culture, still less a recent product of it, as some have foolishly supposed.

This doesn't settle the question of whether there is such a thing, or, if there is, the question of its nature. Four of the papers in this collection (by Dainton, Persson, van Fraassen and van Inwagen) are primarily concerned with the second question; the other two (by Schechtman and Strawson) are primarily concerned with phenomenological and ethical matters; all six allow that there is or could be such a thing as the self.

Barry Dainton opens the book with a 'phenomenalist' account of the nature of the self: an account of the self's existence and persistence that is 'rooted in purely phenomental [i.e. experiental] unity and continuity' (2). This leads him to propose that selves are 'phenomenal substances', on the ground that their identity conditions are stated in experiential or phenomenal terms.

He faces the question of how such a phenomenal-substance self can survive gaps in phenomenal continuity, as in dreamless sleep. His answer (briefly) is that selves are not essentially conscious and are not in that sense *purely* phenomenal continuants. They are, rather, phenomenal-experience-producing systems: 'we trace selves through time via the tracing of capacities for phenomenally continuous experience'.

Can his account still be called 'phenomenalist', given that it now appeals to entities that are not purely phenomenal? Yes, he ingeniously answers: 'I began by advocating a phenomenalist *approach*; I have concluded by advocating a phenomenalist conception of what a self *is*. Whereas Mill maintained that material things were nothing more (or less) than enduring potentials for experience, I am suggesting that this is what we ourselves [i.e. subjects or selves] are. Phenomenalism of this variety is less obviously objectionable than phenomenalism about material things' (23).

Ingmar Persson begins by claiming that I am, essentially, the entity I refer to when I say 'I', and that if there is such a thing as the self, then it is, essentially, the thing I refer to when I say 'I'. He takes it that we can call this entity a 'self', and enquires after its essence. He assumes that it is a persisting thing, and examines the view, popular in analytic philosophy, and in some respects very natural, that what 'I' refers to is nothing less than the whole human organism. He rejects it, mounting a complex argument to show that although we – selves – exist, we are 'not identical to things forming any kind'. We – what we refer to when we say 'I' – are not, for example, instances of the 'natural kind' *human organism.*

How can this be? In a thought-experiment of a familiar sort Persson imagines that the organic materials constituting our bodies – including, in the end, those that constitute our brains – are gradually replaced by inorganic materials while the general form of our experience of ourselves, both internal and external, both mental and non-mental, remains unchanged. Since he accepts the fundamentally empiricist view that the content of our notion of the self, and, hence, the essence of whatever we denote by using the word 'self' or indeed 'I', is wholly given to us in experience, and is therefore untouched by this radical change from orgnaic to inorganic, he concludes that we cannot be identical to human organisms, nor indeed to any other 'natural kind'.[1]

It is no objection to Persson to say that selves are, trivially, members of, instances of, a kind: the kind *self.* What his argument points to, I think, is the idea that the kind *self* is (like the kind *person*) essentially a *functional* kind, not a natural kind.

Where Persson argues that I exist but am not identical to a thing of any (natural) kind, Bas van Fraassen argues, in Sartrean phrase, that 'I exist, but I am not a thing among things. . . . Certainly I have a body and I have thoughts as well as feelings. I have a spatial location as well a place, however, modest, in history. But I am not to be identified with any of this. I am in this world, but not of this world. I am not a thing among things' (87). His achievement is to make this claim seem compelling by appeal-

---

[1] It is true by definition of 'natural kind', in current usage, that the essence of a (non-experiential) natural kind cannot be conclusively known in experience.

ing to nothing more than everyday intuitions – and in a way that
is wholly consistent (though this is no part of van Fraassen's brief)
with a generally materialist or physicalist outlook.

Persson and van Fraassen take very different paths to their conclusions, and the resemblance between their views is in part
extremely superficial. At the same time they share an empiricist
bent, and there are other commonalties. Both think it plain that
a self cannot be identified with a human being considered as a
whole, and both are moved by a fundamental conception of the
self as something whose essence and form of existence (this con-
junction is pleonastic) is far removed from any traditional conception of what a thing or substance is.

The self is nevertheless, and as van Fraassen allows – in so far
as he accepts the term at all – a substance of some kind. It is a
substance in whatever sense being a substance is entailed by being
a subject of experience. It is arguable that there can be no more
secure sense of 'substance' than that (a view with which Kant need
not disagree), and that 'the self' has the following apparently
violently paradoxical characteristic. On the one hand we can
allow that it may be in some sense 'merely' a feature or aspect of
or process in something. On the other hand it must be counted
a substance in any ultimately viable use of that word.

If one's notion of what a substance is doesn't allow for this, then
one needs to adjust it or abandon it. And so one should. The
appearance of paradox is thrown up by a profoundly natural but
metaphysically superficial and ultimately untenable distinction
between objects and their properties, where by 'their properties'
is meant whatever it is about them that makes it true to say that
they are the particular way they are.[2] Alternatively (and ultimately
equivalently) one may say that the appearance of paradox flows
from the ultimately untenable distinction between objects and
processes. On this view all objects are processes, in the final metaphysical analysis. It is metaphysically superficial to insist that a
process needs an object (or set of objects) to go on in or occur
in, and that it is to that extent and at bottom a 'mere' property
or way of being of that object (or set of objects).

It follows from the collapse of the object/process distinction
that all the traditionally favoured candidates for being substances

---

[2]   In the case of concrete objects, then, it is whatever it is in concrete reality that makes
it true to say that they are concretely the particular way they are.

are processes and that the self – the self as 'property-process' – is as good a candidate for being a substance as any. This view is the target of Peter van Inwagen's paper. He defends certain traditional metaphysical categories, in particular the distinction between objects and processes, in order to criticize Strawson's 'theory of the self, of multiple selves, of SESMETS (Subjects of Experience that are Single Mental Things)' (111). He notes that Strawson's rejection of the object/process distinction is essential to his attempt to meet the charge that the concept of a SESMET is an incoherent conflation of the concept *object* and the concept *process*, and, appealing essentially only to premises that most metaphysicians accept, is able to expel Strawson's theory from the court.

During the conference at Reading, van Inwagen, a leading present-day champion of analytic metaphysics, put it to van Fraassen, a leading present-day opponent of all metaphysics, that his – van Fraassen's – own view was itself a piece of metaphysics, for it made a substantive claim about the essential nature of the self, namely, that the self exists but is 'not a thing among things', being 'neither a physical object nor a mental substance or abstract entity, nor any compound thereof'. Van Inwagen also asked van Fraassen whether his account of the self did not make it a substance.

In his published paper van Fraassen replies. 'If being a substance requires only that most of the ordinary things to be said about me are true', then he – the self that is the referent of 'I' – is certainly a substance. He is equally certainly not a substance according to one central traditional metaphysical definition of substance: the self that he is is certainly not something that can exist by itself without dependence on other created beings. According to a second traditional metaphysical definition of substance, however – a 'bearer of attributes', a subject of predication that is not itself predicable, something which 'receives modifications and is not itself a mode' – he is plainly a substance; as he is also given a third traditional definition of a substance, 'the most important one according to Leibniz': *that which acts*. If to say something is a substance is *ipso facto* to make a metaphysical claim, then, van Fraassen says, so be it; but these answers 'derive from ordinary everyday assertions, for which I deny any need for metaphysical underpinning'. They are 'innocuous', fully empirically respectable.

The disagreement about metaphysics depends partly on different understandings of what metaphysics is and many, I think, will seek a middle way. They will agree with van Fraassen – and Hume and Kant – that there is a fundamental sense in which it is fruitless and misguided to make any *knowledge* claims about the ultimate nature of concrete reality that go beyond what can be known in experience and are not *a priori* deducible from what can be known in experience. At the same time they will want to allow, with van Inwagen – and Hume and Kant – not only that we can hold genuinely contentful *beliefs* about and speculate about the ultimate nature of things (in a way that is for us 'natural and inevitable'), but also, and importantly, that in so far as experience does give us knowledge of certain things, we can go on from there to interesting and unobvious necessary truths about the ultimate nature of reality.

In knowing from experience that thoughts occur, for example, thoughts like 'every even number is the sum of two prime numbers' or 'the river is deep and wide', we can not only know that a subject of experience exists, at least at the time of the occurrence of the thought (a piece of metaphysics, if you will). We can also know that the subject is a unitary phenomenon, in some fundamental metaphysical sense, simply in so far as it involves the binding of disparate conceptual elements together in such a way that a genuine, single thought occurs in consciousness.

The tension between the two positions, together with their fundamental compatibility, is illuminated by Kant's discussion of the Paralogisms, in which he famously criticizes the Cartesian 'rational psychologists' for thinking that they can establish with *a priori* certainty that the self or soul is a substance in the traditional metaphysical sense: a bearer of attributes, a subject of predication that is not itself predicable. On the basis of our experience, he says, it is 'quite impossible . . . to determine the manner in which I exist [as a matter of ultimate metaphysical fact], whether it be as substance [or object] or as accident [or property]'.[3] At the same time, however, he grants a sense in which the subject is a substance. His claim here is not just that 'everyone must necessarily regard himself', the conscious subject, 'as a substance', and must regard all episodes of thought or conscious episodes 'as

---

[3] *Critique of Pure Reason* [1781/7], edited by E. Adickes (Berlin: Mayer and Müller, 1889), B420.

being only accidents of his existence, determinations of his state'. He goes further, claiming, strikingly, and rightly, that there is a sense in which the proposition 'The soul is [a] substance' is straightforwardly true, and can be known to be; as van Fraassen agrees.[4]

Marya Schechtman is concerned with the notion of the self that features in the idea of 'being oneself' – the idea that one is in trouble when one is 'not oneself'. She starts from an apparent paradox. On the one hand, we often say that people are not themselves in circumstances that rob them of their self-control. On the other hand we feel that people may be most fully themselves, express their true natures most fully, in just such circumstances. What lies behind both phenomena, she argues, is the fact that 'we can be alienated from our lives' in one way or another. What we need, therefore, is a general account of being oneself, of not being alienated, that can accommodate the insights of both opposing views. Organizing her discussion round Harry Frankfurt's writings on 'wholeheartedness' and the various objections that have been made to it she develops just such an account, 'carefully balancing the demands of self-expression and self-control'.

Galen Strawson argues that there are two main ways in which one may experience oneself: either as a whole human being, or, more restrictedly, as a self. He then distinguishes between various ways in which one may experience oneself as a self. 'Diachronic' people, he proposes, naturally experience their self as something that was there in the (further) past and will be there in the (further) future, 'Episodic' people don't. 'Narrative' personalities construe their lives as a narrative or story of some sort, 'non-Narrative' personalities don't. From this starting point he examines and rejects two currently influential theses, the 'Psychological Narrativity thesis', according to which all normal human beings experience their lives as a narrative or story of some sort, and the 'Ethical Narrativity thesis' (endorsed by Schechtman in her book *The Constitution of Selves*), according to which a richly Narrative outlook is essential to living well, to full personhood.

---

[4]   *Critique of Pure Reason*, A349-50. Kant immediately adds that the sense in which it is true doesn't help the rational psychologists. It doesn't support the claim that the soul or self is a self-subsistent entity, or something that can exist apart from matter; nor, again, can it help one to establish that the soul or self is substance rather than accident in the traditional metaphysical sense.

I warmly thank those who presented their papers at the 2003 Conference, together with Barry Dainton and Marya Schechtman, who made written contributions. I also thank the Analysis Trust and the Centre for Subjectivity Research at the University of Copenhagen for their financial support of the conference; Doug Farland and Katherine Power for helping me out on the day of the conference; John Cottingham for his help in putting the book to bed; and especially Jean Britland of the Reading Philosophy Department for her powerful organizational help.

Galen Strawson
Philosophy Department
University of Reading
January 2005.

CHAPTER 1

THE SELF AND THE PHENOMENAL

Barry Dainton

1. Selves and streams

The foundations of classical physics were shaken when the sixteen year old Einstein imagined being able move as fast as he wished, and setting off in pursuit of a passing ray of light. But although the thought-experiment is justly renowned, its import is by no means self-evident. Why is it, exactly, that a passing ray of light is harder to overtake than a speeding bullet? My topic is the metaphysics of the self, not relativistic physics, and I will not consider these matters further, but a variant of Einstein's thought experiment can shed useful light on this topic.

Suppose, with Einstein, that you can move in any way that you wish, and are constrained only by what is clearly imaginable, rather than by what is nomologically possible. Spend a few moments imagining yourself zooming off to visit distant stars and galaxies, past and future centuries, parallel universes – anywhere that takes your fancy. Then ask yourself this: even so empowered, could you displace yourself in such a way that you leave your *self* behind? Obviously not. The notion is plainly nonsensical; since you and your self are one, where you go it goes, and vice versa. Now consider this: could you move so fast that you leave your *stream of consciousness* behind? The suggestion seems as absurd as its predecessor. We can outlast our current stream of consciousness simply by continuing to exist when unconscious, but we cannot move from it while remaining conscious, no matter how hard we try; any envisaged attempt merely involves an extension of our current stream, not a successful escape from it. Finally, consider a third variant: could your stream of consciousness continue on but fail to take you with it? This is a little trickier, but if we stipulate that as your stream continues on it has much the same subjective character as it usually has, and does not branch, then the answer once again seems perfectly clear. The suggestion that you could cease to exist in such circumstances is as absurd as the suggestion that you ceased to exist at some point during the past few seconds of your conscious life. Whatever else we might be, we are not the kind of being that can cease to exist whilst our consciousness continues on – or so it is natural to suppose.

As is very clear, the connection between ourselves and our streams of consciousness is strong indeed. It is stronger by far than the connections between ourselves and any of the other modes of continuity which characterize our lives, at least if we confine ourselves to the realm of the imaginable. It is easy to imagine ourselves moving from one physical body to another; we need simply imagine our stream of consciousness flowing smoothly on, its subjective character much as per usual – much as it has been for the past five minutes, say – as it is housed in (or sustained by) a succession of numerically different bodies. And as Locke and Kant noted, what goes for bodies and brains also goes for souls and any other self-sustaining thing, whether material or immaterial. It is equally easy to imagine ourselves continuing to exist whilst our psychological states are altered, removed or replaced. Once again, it suffices to imagine that our streams of consciousness flow on as the envisaged changes – in beliefs, memories, intentions and personality traits – take place. (If this does not strike you as obvious, consider how little of your total psychology is impinging on your current experience.)

Not everything that is imaginable is really possible, and no doubt some things that are not imaginable are possible, but the fact that we find it hard to imagine ourselves and our streams of consciousness going their separate ways, and that we find it easy to imagine ourselves surviving any amount of physical and psychological discontinuity, provided our streams of consciousness continue to flow on, is certainly suggestive. It suggests that an account of our existence and persistence conditions that is rooted in purely phenomenal unity and continuity – the sorts of unity and continuity found in our streams of consciousness – will be more compelling, more believable, than any account that is not.

Of course, the notion that we should adopt an experience-based or *phenomenalist* approach to the self is scarcely new, far from it, but the approach has endured a period of comparative neglect, and a number of avenues worth pursuing have yet to be fully explored.[1] Just as there are different ways in which physical

---

[1] 'Phenomenalist' because the approach is rooted in phenomenal consciousness, rather than Mill's reductive proposal for matter and material objects – though, as we shall see, the experience-based approach to the self *can* lead to a position that is analogous in certain respects to this view of Mill's.

and psychological approaches to the self can be developed, there are different ways of developing the phenomenalist approach. In what follows I will outline one such way.

Before doing so, however, I will spend some time on phenomenal unity. This is a sizeable topic in its own right, but my aims are limited. I will be primarily concerned to outline a case for the claim that the unity in our streams of consciousness, both at and over time, is sufficiently robust and autonomous to provide a solid foundation for a credible account of the self. I will also argue that one conception of the source of phenomenal unity is mistaken, and this in itself has implications for the kinds of things selves are, or could be.

2. Phenomenal unity

Some philosophers favour a narrow construal of the term *consciousness*. Starting with the seemingly innocent claim that what differentiates conscious from non-conscious states is that we are 'aware' of the former but not the latter as they occur, they then suggest (more contentiously) that we are aware only of those states that we think about (or attend to, or form beliefs about), and so conclude that our conscious states are restricted to those that we think about (or attend to, or form beliefs about).[2]

I think it is far more natural to construe 'consciousness' in a broader way. As I will be using the term, a state is conscious if there is something that it is like to be in it, irrespective of whether the state is the object of thought, belief or attention. This terminological preference is grounded in phenomenology. Generally speaking, at any one time, my own experience, and hence my own consciousness, is clearly not confined to whatever it is that I am paying attention to or thinking about. If I focus my attention on the fly I see crawling up the wall, my visual experience is not restricted to the fly, I continue to see the surrounding walls and floor – even though I do not explicitly notice them. I also continue to have a wide range of non-visual experiences – auditory experiences of the road works outside, along with bodily and emotional feelings – these too are present despite being largely unnoticed. (If this is not obvious, try to imagine what your experience

---

[2] E.g. Rosenthal (1986).

would be like if it *were* limited, at any given time, to whatever you happen to be paying attention to or thinking about!) I take all these background experiences to be constituent parts of my current total state of consciousness.

Let us turn to the main issue, and start by considering synchronic unity. From a phenomenological perspective, it is perfectly obvious that our typical streams of consciousness are unified at any given time. Our conscious thoughts and mental images do not occur separately from our bodily sensations, our bodily sensations do not occur separately from our visual experiences, our visual experiences do not occur separately from our auditory, tactile or olfactory experiences. On the contrary, all our experiences, of all types, typically occur together, in unified experiential ensembles. This unity or togetherness is itself something we experience. Focus your attention on one of your current bodily sensations, and then consider just how this sensation is related to part of your visual field, or something you can hear (or a mental image, or your current conscious thinking, etc.). Clearly, the bodily sensation and auditory experience are occurring together within your overall state of consciousness, and this togetherness is itself experienced: there is something distinctive that it is like to experience these two experiences together, rather than separately. This experienced togetherness – this *co-consciousness* as I will call it – does not, it should be noted, consist in a separate experiential ingredient, with its own distinctive phenomenal character; there is no additional experiential element occurring between the bodily sensation and the visual content. There is simply the bodily sensation and the sound, experienced together. Precisely the same relationship connects your bodily sensation with your visual experience, and your visual experience with your conscious thoughts. Quite generally, each and every part of a typical state of consciousness is co-conscious with each and every other part.

If we confine ourselves to the phenomenal level, and concern ourselves only with structures and features discernible in our consciousness, rather than their underlying mechanisms and causes, is there anything more to be said on the topic of synchronic unity? According to what I call the *Simple Conception* of consciousness, there is not. On this view, experiential unity is a primitive feature of consciousness. Unified states of consciousness simply consist of experiences related to one another by co-consciousness, and that is all there is to be said.

3. Pure awareness & bare loci

There is another a way of thinking about the synchronic unity of consciousness, one that has broader implications. The position I have in mind is a variant of the doctrine that consciousness requires, or is a form of, awareness. Not awareness in the form of belief-acquisition or conscious thought, but rather awareness in the form of *perception* (or *sensing*), where the latter is construed in the manner of the naïve realist, as an unmediated apprehension of an object or content. According to what I will call the *naïve perceptual* (NP) conception of consciousness, every episode of experiencing involves two components: an act or process of apprehension, and the various contents falling under, or apprehended by, this act. All the phenomenal qualities that feature in our consciousness reside at the level of content, and these qualities only become conscious when they are apprehended; the act of apprehension itself is devoid of qualities, and in this sense 'pure'. The 'contents' of consciousness thus include occurrent thoughts, mental images and emotional feelings, as well as the deliverances of our various senses. Since the contents falling under a subject's awareness can include peripheral or background elements in our experience, the NP-conception should not be equated with the 'narrow' conception of consciousness mentioned above.[3]

Given our present concerns, the NP-conception has a double interest. It yields an intuitively appealing account of the unity of consciousness: experiential contents are unified, or co-conscious, only if they fall under a single act of pure sensory awareness. But it also points towards a conception of what selves are. Perhaps conscious selves are nothing more than centres (or loci) of pure awareness. Following Mark Johnston (1987), I will call this the *bare locus* view of the self.

This view does have some appeal. I suspect many of us can make sense of the suggestion that we could, in extremis, be reduced to nothing more than a point of pure apprehension, gazing outward, all senses keenly alert but detecting nothing.

---

[3] So-called 'act-object' conceptions of consciousness were commonplace in the 19th and early 20th centuries, but versions of the doctrine continue to flourish among contemporary 'higher-order sense' theorists, see for example Armstrong (1997) and Lycan (1997); also Lockwood (1989: 162–3).

Nonetheless, when considered seriously, the doctrine quickly begins to look suspect.

Since a bare locus is nothing but a point-centre of featureless apprehension, there can clearly be nothing that it is like to *be* a bare locus in the absence of apprehended contents. The condition of being a bare locus that is not apprehending anything would be subjectively indistinguishable from not existing at all. Can we really make sense of the idea that an entity such as this could exist? Is the concept of a bare locus any more intelligible than the concept of a bare particular, the featureless *something* that allegedly remains when all the properties of an object are removed from it? I cannot see that it is. Nor does it help if we suppose that bare loci can only exist when apprehending some content or other. For again, given that bare loci have no qualitative contribution to make whatsoever, what reason do we have for supposing that anything about our conscious experience would be in any way different if they were absent? This invites the reply: 'Without the bare loci there would be no one to experience anything, and hence no experience!' But this does not take us any further, since what is in question is precisely how this could be possible![4]

Since bare loci are nothing more or less than centres of pure apprehension, these considerations also weigh against the NP-conception. However, the case against the latter would be stronger if the Simple Conception could be shown to have the resources to account for the intuitive appeal of the perceptual model. Why, if it is erroneous, can the latter seem so compelling?

Although the full story is complex, three of the more significant influences are not too difficult to discern. First and most obviously, much of our ordinary experience *is* perceptual, and much of our perceptual experience has a presentational character: the things we see and hear seem to be 'out there' in the world, as opposed to 'in here' with our thoughts, feelings and bodily experiences. The NP-conception misdescribes the reality of the situation – in our case at least, there is a definite something that it is like to *be* an observer of an external world – but it is no means a completely erroneous view of consciousness.

A second source of the perceptual model's appeal lies in the phenomenology of attention. We can attend to any part of our

---

[4]   See Dainton (2002) for more on this theme.

experience, and when we do so it often seems like we are 'seeing' what is there for the first time. And in a sense we are: when some feature of what is there comes to our notice for the first time. But again, ordinary forms of attending have their own qualitative character, unlike the NP-theorist's pure apprehension, and are directed at only some of a subject's experiences, not all of them.

Thirdly, and perhaps most importantly, there are the so-called 'fringe feelings' that accompany our sensory experiences and conscious thoughts. Think of what it is like to see a face and know that you have seen it before, without being able to quite place it. Compare this with what it is like to know that a certain word just isn't right, or *is* right. Or think of what it is like to carry out a task with the reassuring feeling that everything is proceeding as it should – or with the feeling that it isn't. In each of these cases (and in many others of the same genre) there is a feeling or intuition with a quite specific character, a feeling whose significance is entirely unambiguous, but one that does not possess a qualitative character of a sensory kind – they have no definite spatial location, size or colour, for instance. Such feelings are easily overlooked, but when our attention is drawn to them it soon becomes apparent that they are commonplace; indeed, they are significant ingredients in our overall consciousness.[5]

As for their relevance to the topic in hand, when we ponder our natures as conscious beings most of us have no difficulty in accepting the claim that there is something more to us than the various contents we are currently aware of, and equally the claim that we are active apprehending *somethings* that are distinct from these contents. Having recognized the existence and significance of fringe feelings we can account for this without recourse to the additional (and introspectively invisible) level of consciousness posited by the NP-theorist. Such claims strike us as plausible because there is a sense in which they are true: there is indeed an additional something in consciousness; not a point-centre of pure awareness, but simply fringe feelings of various types, some more ubiquitous than others. Among the most significant in the present context are the feelings associated with conditions such as these: *being in a state of readiness, opening or straining one's senses, being pre-*

---

[5] William James' exploration of the fringe is to be found in the 'Principles of Tendency' section of the *Principles*. For more on the topic see Epstein (2000) and especially Mangan (2001).

pared for the unexpected, being determined or resolute, potency: having the sense that one is mentally or physically energized, that one is equipped for the task in hand, that one is about to act. It is, I suggest, the presence of these and similar feelings that, to a large extent, gives rise to the sense that we are active apprehending subjects. What else could possibly be needed? Imagine your consciousness being gradually emptied of all content until all that remains is a single solitary fringe feeling: *being ready for whatever happens next.* If we try to imagine ourselves existing in the form of a 'pure locus of awareness', don't we end up imagining something along these lines? If so, 'pure' does not really mean 'devoid of all content', it simply means 'devoid of all *non-fringe* content'.

There is a good deal more than could be said about this, but perhaps I have said enough to demonstrate that adopting the Simple Conception does not mean embracing a phenomenologically impoverished or obviously inadequate view of our consciousness. A recognizable picture of the latter can be constructed from experiential elements – of all kinds – related to one another by the primitive joining relation of co-consciousness.

4. Phenomenal continuity

Let us move on to streams of consciousness proper, and consider the ways in which their constituent parts are unified over time, from moment to moment.

The first point to note is the relevance of the distinction between narrow and broad conceptions of consciousness. From the narrow perspective it is implausible to suppose that consciousness is stream-like. Suppose it were the case that we are conscious only of what we are paying attention to; since our attention often flits quickly from one thing to another, and sometimes we are not attending to anything at all, our consciousness would exhibit a corresponding degree of discontinuity. But when matters are viewed from the broad perspective the situation is very different. Generally speaking, we are continually conscious throughout our waking (and dreaming) hours, in the sense that at each moment during such periods we are experiencing *something*. We may not be thinking about what we are experiencing, we may not be attending to what we are experiencing, we may not be conscious in a self-conscious way, but experience is there nonetheless. If this were not so, we would not have the impression of being continuously awake, nor would we have the impression that the world is continuously *there* before us in the way that it generally seems to be.

Our ordinary streams of consciousness may usually be composed of continuous (gap-free) stretches of experience, but their unity is more far-reaching. Yes, we experience continuously, but continuity is also something we experience, all the time. Think of what it like to view the passing countryside from the window of a moving train: trees, roads, buildings – you watch them all sliding by. This smooth continuous movement is something you actually *see*, not merely infer. It is much the same if you walk round a room, or turn your head; or listen to a rising violin tone, or your friend's conversation (or your own inner soliloquy) while enjoying the burning heat of a chilli pepper on your tongue; or do no more than acknowledge the relentless passing of time while gazing, unthinking, at an open expanse of sky. Quite generally, throughout our waking and dreaming hours, and in all regions of our consciousness, we are directly experiencing change or persistence. Our ordinary experience is not merely continuous, continuity is a ubiquitous presence within our experience.

Recognizing the two-sided character of phenomenal continuity is one thing, explaining precisely what it involves, even at the purely phenomenal level, is quite another, and this is not the place to attempt it. All I will do is outline a case for a strong constraint on any adequate account of phenomenal continuity. As is customary, I will use the (less than optimal) term 'specious present' to refer to those brief phases of our streams of consciousness during which we are directly aware of change and persistence.[6] Since a specious present has some (apparent) temporal depth, it has (seemingly) earlier and later parts; and since the transition between these parts is directly experienced, the parts are *phenomenally connected* – they are co-conscious, but diachronically rather than synchronically. If, as seems plausible, we regard a stream of consciousness as being composed of a succession of specious presents, a question arises. How are neighbouring specious presents in the same stream of consciousness related to one another? Two positions can be distinguished:

Streams of consciousness are *partially connected*: there are diachronic phenomenal connections only within individual specious presents.

Streams of consciousness are *fully connected*: there are diachronic phenomenal connections within and between specious presents.

Although several prominent accounts of the diachronic structure of consciousness reject full connectedness in favour of partial connectedness, there are good reasons for doing the reverse.

Consider what it is like to hear a plane passing overhead: an ongoing roar that endures without interruption for a several minutes, before fading. Below is a pictorial representation of a few seconds of this experience (Figure 1):

This line does not reflect all aspects of the experience – e.g., the changes in volume and timbre – but it captures perfectly the feature which interests us: its sheer continuity. As the plane passes, we hear an uninterrupted flow of sound, with no seams or gaps of any kind.

Now suppose, as some have alleged, that our streams of consciousness are composed of non-overlapping pulses, each the duration of a single specious present, and that the impression we have that our consciousness is fully continuous is due to qualitative similarities between neighbouring pulses together with short-term memory-impressions.[7] It may seem that this theory can accommodate and account for the experience of phenomenal continuity, in the way depicted in Figure 2:

---

[6]   How brief is 'brief'? Perhaps only around one second, or even a little less. The shortest interval within which typical human subjects can discern distinct temporally ordered stimuli (in all sense modalities) is around 30 milliseconds – Pöppel (1985) – this puts a lower bound on our specious presents, construed as temporal cross-sections of our entire streams of consciousness.

[7]   Sprigge (1981, ch. 1) and Whitehead (1929) advocate this simple model, but the more complex accounts of time-consciousness developed by Broad (1938) and Husserl (1991) also reject full connectedness, and do so in an even more dramatic fashion. On these views, the specious present is a momentary experience with a content that *represents* a temporal interval, and does so in such a way that it appears to possess genuine temporal depth. In effect, accounts such as this merely *multiply* the number of discrete pulses, for it remains the case that there are no genuine experiential links between successive specious presents. See Dainton (2003) for a more detailed discussion, especially of Husserl's account.

Here each of P_1-P_4 represents adjoining specious presents, each containing a brief pulse of sound; the continuity of the sound is due to the fact that there are no gaps between the pulses. What more could possibly be required? Actually, a good deal. There are inter-experiential relations that the pulse theory ignores or misrepresents, a few of which are depicted in Figure 3.

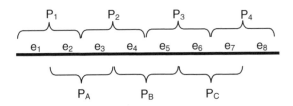

Here, e_1, e_2, e_3 ... e_8 are the earlier and later phases of the specious presents P_1, P_2, P_3 and P_4. The pulse theory adequately captures some inter-experiential relations, e.g., e_1 is experienced as flowing into e_2, and e_3 is experienced as flowing into e_4. But what of e_2 and e_3? Or e_4 and e_5? Since by hypothesis these occur in distinct pulses, the transitions between them cannot be directly experienced. But this is manifestly at odds with the phenomenology. When listening to the passing plane what we hear is a seamless flow: e_1-flowing-into-e_2-flowing-into-e_3- ... and so on. The diachronic phenomenal connections indicated by all the lower brackets have precisely the same phenomenal character as those indicated by the upper brackets – all seem equally real. And what goes for this auditory experience goes for the successive brief phases of our entire streams of consciousness. Since it denies this, the pulse theory is manifestly inadequate to the phenomena. The same will be true of any account of the diachronic structure of our streams of consciousness which fails to accept that our streams of consciousness are fully connected. There are direct diachronic phenomenal connections between *all* the adjoining brief phases of a single stream of consciousness. Unless we recognize this we cannot hope to do justice to the two-sided character of phenomenal continuity.

Or so I think it reasonable to believe. There is, however, a line of reasoning that casts doubt on the full-connectedness constraint, and before moving on I will indicate where I think it goes astray. Here is one way of formulating what I have in mind:

The Cut Argument Suppose that at precisely noon today, just as you are about to cross a busy street, you are vaporized, instantaneously, by a devastatingly powerful laser beam. Although your annihilation brings your stream of consciousness to an immediate halt, it does not affect in the slightest the character of your experience leading up to this event. How could it? Are we to suppose that your pre-noon experience is affected by events that have yet to occur, via some mysterious channel of backwards causation? Assuming not, it seems that your experience leading up to the moment of your annihilation is just as it would have been if the trigger on the laser had not been pressed, and you had continued about your business as per usual. The point generalizes. There is nothing special about you, and nothing special about that particular time. Any of us *could* be annihilated at any of our waking moments, and this could occur without impinging on the character of the immediately preceding experiences. And we can take a further step. We are all familiar with the sceptical claim that 'everything could be just as it is now even if the entire universe only came into existence five minutes ago'. If this is right, then surely the universe could have come into being five *seconds* ago – or even five milliseconds – without affecting the character of our experience now. This also applies to everyone, at all times. Putting these points together, and bearing in mind the fact that the 'cuts' could come anywhere in any stream, it is clear that the phenomenal character of any short stretch of experience *E* is logically independent of both later and earlier experiences in the same stream of consciousness: *E* could be just as it is, phenomenologically speaking, if the experiences immediately before and after it did not exist. It follows that a stream of consciousness consists of a succession of experiential phases, each of which is entirely self-contained and isolated, at least on the phenomenal level, from its immediate neighbours.

While the Cut Argument can seem persuasive, we have already seen that if our streams of consciousness really did consist of successions of isolated, phenomenally self-contained phases, then our experience could not exhibit the continuity that it typically does. So the Cut Argument must contain a flaw – but where?

The error is not difficult to discern. It is logically possible for a short-lived subject – a *two-second subject*, say – to have a stream of consciousness which very closely resembles the two-seconds of consciousness that you (or anyone else) has just enjoyed. The mistake comes in supposing that this stream-phase is exactly the same as the corresponding stretch of your experience in *all* phenomenal respects. There are differences, and the differences are such that putting a succession of self-contained phases end to end, as it were, would *not* result in a stream of consciousness of the kind we typically enjoy.

To illustrate, suppose you listen to someone repeatedly playing a C-major scale on a piano: *C-D-E-F-G-A-B-C.* . . . Let us also suppose that on some distant (but logically possible) world a short-lived duplicate of you comes into being, in an exactly similar room, containing a similar piano, and hears just the *D* segment of a similarly pitched C-scale, before ceasing to exist. Would your ephemeral duplicate's *D*-experience exactly resemble your own? In intrinsic phenomenal respects, perhaps. The auditory qualities of the *D*-tone you each experience might be indistinguishable; you might also both hear *D* while experiencing a short-term acoustic memory-image of a preceding *C*, and an anticipation of hearing an *E*. But so far as diachronic phenomenal *relations* are concerned, your duplicate's experience cannot exactly resemble yours. You hear *C*-running into-*D*, and *D*-running into-*E*, but since neither *C* nor *E* are experienced by your duplicate, neither are these phenomenal relations. Hence in one key respect, your duplicate's experience is necessarily different from your own.

Once diachronic phenomenal connections are brought into the picture it is obvious where the Cut Argument goes astray. An experience's non-relational phenomenal characteristics may be logically independent of what comes before or after, but it is otherwise with regard to its relational features. Once this is recognized, it is evident that a *stream* of consciousness does not consist of a succession of self-contained chunks or pulses of experience, laid end to end like a row of bricks. Or at least, if we do think of a stream in this way, we must not forget the cement which holds the bricks together. In addition to phenomenal connections *within* stream-phases, we must also recognize the phenomenal connections *between* them. The plausibility of the Cut Argument derives from a conception of the diachronic features of consciousness that is as incomplete as it is impoverished. By way of a final illustration of this point, consider Figure 4 below, where four brief stream-segments are shown.

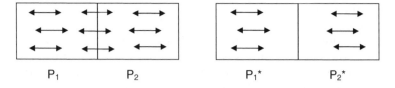

$$P_1 \qquad\qquad P_2 \qquad\qquad\qquad P_1{}^* \qquad\qquad P_2{}^*$$

Thanks to the presence of the diachronic phenomenal connections linking P_1 and P_2, this pair of stream-phases form a phenomenally continuous stretch of experience. In this instance, the depicted spatial proximity between these phases accurately reflects experiential reality. It is otherwise with respect to $P_1{}^*$ and $P_2{}^*$. Given the absence of phenomenal connections between these phases, they might as well belong to different subjects, or exist in different universes. In short, the Cut Argument presupposes that our ordinary experience is as depicted on the right, when in reality, it is as shown on the left.

There is, of course, more to be said on this topic. Just how long is a specious present? What sort of experiential connection gives rise to diachronic phenomenal relations? But we need not address these matters here.[8] For present purposes it is sufficient that any adequate account of phenomenal continuity must recognize that own typical streams of consciousness are fully, rather than merely partially, connected.

5. Consciousness and self: a parting of ways

The claim that experiences within a typical stream of consciousness are bound together by purely phenomenal relations has solid phenomenological support. We do not need to look beyond the phenomenal to determine which experiences belong to which streams: simultaneous experiences are 'co-streamal', part of the same stream, only if they are related by synchronic co-consciousness; non-simultaneous experiences are co-streamal only if they are diachronically co-conscious, either *directly*, i.e., they occur within a single phenomenal present, or *indirectly*, i.e., they are part of a chain of overlapping specious presents.

---

[8]   The simplest way of accommodating full connectedness is to permit neighbouring specious presents to overlap by sharing common parts, in the manner advocated Russell (1984) and Foster (1979). See Dainton (2000, 2003) for more detailed treatments of these topics.

What use is all this in regard to the self? Given the intimacy of the connection between selves and streams of consciousness we noted at the outset, and using 'consubjective' to mean 'belongs to the same self or subject', the following seems plausible:

The S-thesis: Co-streamal experiences are consubjective.

Bearing in mind what has just been noted concerning stream membership, we also have:

The C-thesis: Experiences that are co-conscious, directly or indirectly, are consubjective.

This is fine as far as it goes, but it doesn't take us very far. Any attempt to construct an account of the self appealing only to phenomenal relations faces an obvious hurdle. While we are undeniably conscious some of the time, we are not conscious all of the time. Or at least, if we are conscious all of the time, this is by no means obvious. It seems to most of us that we lose consciousness completely at least once every twenty four hours, when we slide off into dreamless sleep. If this is right, then a typical person can expect to have several thousand distinct streams of consciousness during the course of their life.

There are two fundamentally different ways of approaching the 'gap' problem available to the phenomenalist, each rooted in a different conception of the kind of thing a self is. Each of these conceptions is a way of developing the idea that a self is essentially a thing that has experiences. Here is the first:

The Essentially Conscious Self [ECS]: a self is a thing whose nature it is to *be* conscious; a self is experiencing at every moment at which it exists. A self cannot lose consciousness and continue to exist.

According to this conception, selves cannot exist when unconscious, and so they cannot persist through periods of unconsciousness. Given the seemingly intermittent nature of our conscious lives, advocates of ECS have two options. They can adhere to the common sense view of things, accept that we each have a succession of distinct streams of consciousness, and provide some account of what renders such streams consubjective. Alternatively, they can take the more radical option of denying the appearances, and hold that a self has but a single uninterrupted stream of consciousness.

Neither of these options is very palatable. The only obvious way of developing the 'many streams' approach is to hold that distinct streams of consciousness are consubjective in virtue of some feature that is internal to the streams. But what feature? Do all your streams of consciousness have some unique phenomenal feature that could serve to mark them out as yours and yours alone? Perhaps on occasion, but all of the time? Every day? As an infant? It seems unlikely.[9] The 'single stream' approach fares little better. Advocates of this doctrine face a dilemma. They can embrace the hard-to-believe option of holding that typical human selves exist for no more than a few hours,[10] or they can follow Descartes in denying that we ever truly lose consciousness during the normal course of our lives – what seems like dreamless sleep is really low-level consciousness that we are later unable to recall. While this suggestion may not be so absurd as to merit the scorn habitually heaped upon it, as things stand it is at best speculative – and of course Descartes was not acquainted with modern day general anaesthetics.[11]

Phenomenalists are not obliged to opt for any of these proposals. The notion that selves are essentially experiencers can be construed in a different way:

The Potentially Conscious Self [PCS]: a self is a thing whose nature it is to be *capable* of being conscious; a self has the *capacity* for consciousness at every moment at which it exists, and it possesses this capacity essentially. A self can lose consciousness provided it retains the potential to be consciousness.

[9] Not everyone would agree with this verdict: see Nathan (1997) for a recent defence of the similarity approach. Nathan is sympathetic to the view that our overall states of consciousness are always characterized by a *tone* or *flavour*, of a subtle and easily overlooked kind, and that since we each of us have a unique phenomenal essence, as it were, one that is unlike anyone else's, this feature can serve to distinguish our own experiences, whenever and wherever they might occur. This contention is not susceptible to direct empirical refutation, but equally, it lacks direct empirical support, and so far as I can see, the considerations which might incline one to accept the speculation are outweighed by those point in the other direction.

[10] Strawson favours the more radical position that selves only endure for a second or so, on the grounds that 'strongly unified' or 'hiatus free' episodes of experience only last this long. I agree that episodes of what Strawson calls 'Self-experience . . .' – which he describes as '. . . the experience that people have of themselves as being, specifically, a mental presence' (1999: 104) – are usually short-lived. But this is compatible with consciousness in the broad sense being continuous, and strongly unified from moment to moment, for much longer periods. See also Dainton (2000: §5.2).

[11] There are further radical options: to hold that interruptions in a subject's consciousness exist in objective but not subjective time, the Berkeleian view also defended by Evans (1970) – or to deny that selves exist in time at all – see Robinson (forthcoming).

This conception retains the tight link between selves and consciousness, but has the merit of conforming to the common sense view that consciousness is something that we can lose and regain. Also, since on this view a self continues to exist when unconscious, we can simply say that what renders distinct streams consubjective is the fact that they belong to the same self – thus avoiding the untempting stratagems forced upon those who subscribe to the doctrine of the essentially conscious self.

But while it brings definite advantages, the PCS doctrine faces difficulties of its own. What manner of existence do non-conscious selves enjoy? If conscious and non-conscious selves are instances of the same kind of being, *what* kind of being?

6. Phenomenal substances

One way forward is to start with the general notion of 'a thing which can have or produce experiences', and specify the identity conditions of such things relying solely on the intimate relationship between selves and their experiences encapsulated in the S- and C-theses. The following concept provides a point of departure:

> **Experience Producer** [EP]: any object or system that can directly produce experience in response to external or internal changes.

This characterization is neutral with regard to structure and constitution. Human brains are EPs, but so are feline brains (probably), as are immaterial souls, if there are or could be such things. What makes something an experience producer is the capacity, grounded in natural law, to produce unified experience – it is this capacity that matters, nothing else. As we know from our own case, such a capacity can be activated by external influences (as in perception), or as a consequence of internal processes (mental images, memories, internal dialogue, etc.).

The concept of an EP is a useful starting point, but it does not provide us with everything we need. Most significantly, it does not provide us with a conception of an entity whose persistence conditions are framed in phenomenal terms. Being an EP is a non-essential temporary property of many of the objects that possess the relevant capacities. Most human brains are EPs, but their identity conditions are biological rather than experiential, and a given brain can gain and lose the capacity to produce experience. Since selves of the potentially conscious variety cannot do likewise, identifying selves with EPs of this type is not an option. And of course, we want to leave room, conceptually at least, for a single self to be sustained by a succession of such supporting systems.

There is a further difficulty of a different kind. Suppose it were the case that your auditory and visual experiences were the products of two distinct neural systems, each of which is capable of functioning independently of the other. Given that a typical field of auditory experience is a synchronically unified ensemble, and a typical field of visual experience likewise, by the lights of the definition supplied above, each of these neural systems would count as an EP in its own right. But clearly, EPs like this are not selves, they are merely parts of selves.

Noting these deficiencies points the way forward. It would be a mistake simply to equate selves with EPs, but it may nonetheless be possible to state the identity conditions of the former in terms of relationships among the latter, at and over time. We can start thus:

> **E-linkage:** at any time t, one or more EPs are *E-linked* if and only if (i) they are active, and the experiences they are producing are mutually synchronically co-conscious, or (ii) they are not active, but if they were, the experiences that would result would be mutually synchronically co-conscious.

E-linked EPs are akin to groups of 'co-targeted' spotlights: the members of such a group need not be turned on, but if they *were*, the resulting light-rays would converge on the same spatial location. In similar fashion, the members of a group of E-linked EPs need not all be active and producing experience, but if they are, all the resulting experiences are co-conscious. (I allow a single EP to be E-linked so as to accommodate the case of a self composed of just one EP at a given time.)

It is certainly very plausible to suppose that E-linked EPs are consubjective, and it is hard to see how normally functioning EPs at a given time could be consubjective unless they were E-linked. Since we are interested in *all* the EPs that belong to any one self at a given time, it will prove convenient to have a label for such collections:

> **E-system:** any maximal collection of E-linked EPs at a given time t compose an E-system.

A collection C of E-linked EPs is less than maximal if at the time in question there are EPs that are not in C but that are nonetheless E-linked to the members of C.

We now have the beginnings of a plausible account of how EPs at a given time must be related if they are to belong to, or compose, a single self. We still need an account, in phenomenal terms, of how EPs at different times must be related in order to be consubjective. Here we can rely on the diachronic aspect of the C-thesis, on the fact that experiences can be co-conscious over time as well as at times. As we saw earlier, the temporal depth of diachronic co-consciousness is not great – only experiences within a single specious present are so related – but the relationship is just as real as its synchronic counterpart. Putting this relationship to work, it is plausible to hold that E-systems existing at different times that can contribute to the same specious present belong to the same self. So too, over the longer term, E-systems that can contribute to the same extended stream of consciousness belong to the same self. More formally:

(1) E-systems S_1 at t_1 and S_2 at t_2 are *directly streamally linked* if, and only if, (i) both systems are active and producing experiences that are directly diachronically co-conscious, or (ii) if both systems *were* active, the experiences they would produce would be directly diachronically co-conscious.

The notion of 'direct streamal linkage' is simply the diachronic counterpart of E-linkage. As for the longer term:

(2) E-systems S_1 at t_1 and S_2 at t_2 are *indirectly streamally linked* if, and only if, they are at either end of a chain of E-systems, the neighbouring members of which are directly streamally linked.

Together, (1) and (2) allow us to state the conditions under which a single E-system persists through time:

(3) E-systems S_1 at t_1 and S_2 at t_2 are the same enduring E-system if, and only if, S_1 and S_2 are streamally linked, directly or indirectly.

Alternatively, for those who prefer to think of persistence in a four-dimensional framework:

(3)′ E-systems S_1 at t_1 and S_2 at t_2 are temporal parts of the same perduring E-system if, and only if, S_1 and S_2 are streamally linked, directly or indirectly.

Bringing these formulations somewhat closer to home:

(4) Members of a collection of experiences are consubjective if, and only if, they are produced by EPs belonging to the same E-system.

And finally:

(5) E-systems can be regarded as a distinctive kind of entity: *phenomenal substances.*

(6) E-systems and selves are one and the same.[12]

A simple picture underlies these formulations: the tracing of selves through time via the tracing of capacities for phenomenally continuous experience. Our brains are (probably) E-systems for most if not all of their careers, but the identity conditions of the latter are sufficiently general so as to permit a wide range of very different entities also to count as E-systems. There is no need for the relevant systems to be organic, physical or spatially continuous: a succession of immaterial souls would constitute an E-system if they were capable of sustaining a single stream of consciousness. Since E-systems have distinctive and well-defined identity conditions, there is no reason why they should not be regarded as perfectly respectable objects or substances in their own right. Since these identity conditions are framed in experiential terms, to call them *phenomenal* substances seems appropriate.

We could stop here, but a case can be made for taking a further step. E-systems are composed of EPs, and although EPs all have at least one thing in common – the capacity to produce experience – in other respects they may be very different. It would surely be unwise to rule out even the possibility that conscious beings may come in very different forms. We can cut through these variations, and isolate what is common to all conscious beings, at least of the PCS variety, by defining their identity conditions in terms of what is common to all EPs. Rather than taking experience-producing *objects* as our basic ingredient, we take certain *properties* of these objects. As for the sort of property, there is only one candidate: the property common to all EPs: the power to generate experiences.

It is as easy to formulate a set of identity conditions in these new terms as it was in the old. In fact, we can keep the formula-

---

[12] Endurantists need not regard themselves as being numerically identical with any particular collection of EPs – they can regard E-systems as *composed* or *constituted* from particular collections of EPs, a view which permits an E-system to be made up of different EPs than it actually is at any one time – the definition of an E-system leaves this option open. Most perdurantists will be happy to accept the identity.

tions and simply interpret them in a new way. To start with, we allow the abbreviation 'EP' to refer to *experiential power* rather than *experience producer*. An EP in the new sense is simply a nomological capacity, no doubt usually possessed by some object or system, to produce experience of one or more kinds in response to appropriate triggering circumstances. Next, we re-interpret the definitions of 'E-linkage' and 'E-system' in the same way. An E-system is now a maximal collection of experiential powers, unified in their ability to produce experiences that are co-conscious. To avoid confusion I will henceforth use the expression *E*-system* to mark the change. The persistence of these systems can be defined as in (1)–(3), in terms of the capacity to produce extended streams of experience. We can then draw revised versions of our earlier conclusions:

(5)* E*-systems can be regarded as a distinctive kind of entity: *phenomenal substances.*

(6)* E*-systems and selves are one and the same.

Although the E*-proposal has some counterintuitive features – thinking of ourselves as nothing more than a collection of properties may take a bit of getting used to – it also has a good deal to recommend it. The account is general enough to apply to most of the things we might ever be tempted to call 'selves', it tells us what all these entities have in common, and it is permissive enough to permit a single self to survive the most radical transformations, provided its capacity for experience is not eliminated.

The account combines generality with a degree of specificity. The most obvious way of defining the identity conditions of an arbitrary experiential power P is in terms of three components: (i) the kind of experience P produces when activated, (ii) the type of circumstance that will trigger P, (iii) the ground of P. The 'ground' of a particular token capacity is what possesses that capacity. Some capacities are grounded in objects, or in certain (usually non-dispositional) properties of an object, others may be grounded in nothing more than regions of space – electrical fields can be construed thus. Our own EPs appear to be grounded in various regions of our brains, but there may be selves whose EPs are differently grounded. By virtue of the fact that EPs *have* grounds, and that differently grounded EPs will usually have different triggering conditions, there is plenty of scope for the detailed descriptions of different selves to vary. But of course, if systems of very different kinds can possess or constitute EPs, variations of this sort are only to be expected. And these differences in detail are quite compatible with all selves having the same high-level existence and persistence conditions.

Some may object: 'The E*-theory may have certain merits, but it signally fails to do justice to the fact that, whatever else we may be, we are definitely *things*, and whatever else they may be, clusters of properties are not things.' This objection overlooks the fact that on one standard metaphysical view non-abstract objects of all kinds are nothing more than clusters of properties! But setting aside this point, in one respect the objection is warranted. The claim that E*-systems are substances, albeit of the phenomenal variety, sits uneasily with the doctrine that the distinguishing mark of a genuine substance is that it does not depend for its existence on anything else. But while it may well be that no E*-systems have this degree of independence, it is worth noting that there is another traditional criterion of genuine object-hood: unity. The grounds of an E*-system need not exhibit material or spatial cohesion, but it remains the case that unity is the defining characteristic of E*-systems. To qualify as members of such a system experiential powers must be capable generating co-conscious experiences. And as we saw earlier, the unity to be found in our consciousness is very real indeed.

7. Selves and subjects

So much for the E*-account in bare outline. There are many details to be filled in, and further issues to explore. EPs are dispositional properties; there are several competing accounts of such properties, all with implications for the kind of entity E*-systems might be. We need an account of the different ways in which capacities can be rendered inoperative – how does deep sleep differ from death? How do we draw the boundaries? Can an E*-system undergo fission? If so, what happens to a self which divides? Even if our essential cores are nothing more than clusters of experiential capacities, there is more to a typical self than its essential core; we also have bodies and psychologies, and we need some account of how E*-systems are related to these. These are all interesting topics, but I cannot hope to do justice to any of them here, so will conclude with a few general observations.

There is a sense in which things have come full circle. I began by advocating a phenomenalist *approach* to the self; I have concluded by advocating a phenomenalist conception of what a self *is*. Whereas Mill maintained that material things were nothing more (or less) than enduring potentials for experience, I am suggesting that this is what we ourselves are. Phenomenalism of this variety is less obviously objectionable than phenomenalism about material things.

I have not suggested any limit on the kind of experiential potential that is needed to sustain a self in being. This omission was deliberate. As noted at the outset, it is hard to envisage one's stream of consciousness flowing on but failing to take oneself with it, and this holds irrespective of how broad or deep one's stream is. If I imagine the capabilities of my own E*-system being progressively diminished, with the result that my consciousness becomes progressively simpler in character, it seems obvious that I continue to exist, even if I am incapable of experiencing anything other than a few primitive bodily sensations. In the absence of actual experience, the continued existence of the capacities for such experience is enough to keep me in existence – or so I am inclined to believe.

Not everyone will find this minimalist approach to survival congenial, but those who do must address this question: When your experiential capabilities are reduced to a very low level, do you remain a *self*? The idea that you might remain in existence but fail to remain a self may seem very odd. If by 'self' we simply mean 'subject of consciousness' or 'thing that can have experience', then the idea is nonsensical. But there are those who equate selves with beings who are capable of being aware of themselves *as* selves.

Self-awareness comes in different forms, but there is no need to attempt a inventory here: anyone reduced to the minimal level of sentience will be incapable of self-awareness in any interesting sense. So anyone attracted by the minimalist approach to survival *and* a high-level reflexive notion of selfhood should be prepared to acknowledge that they are not essentially selves, only subjects, and that as such they share their identity conditions with more primitive beings (though of course more advanced sentient beings, if such exist, are subjects of experience too).

Irrespective of whether we think of ourselves subjects or selves, we should try to think of ourselves in the right way. We are things that are capable of *having* experiences. What exactly does this involve? If the various doctrines I have been propounding here are along the right lines, subjects are not things which passively apprehend their experiences, nor are they things which experiences impinge upon. They are things which *make* or *generate* experiences. This too can seem somewhat odd. But then, given the character of our experiences, of the experiences we make, it is not surprising that this seems odd. As has often been observed, selves are rather elusive.[13]

References

Armstrong, D. (1997). 'What Is Consciousness?' in Block *et al.*

Block, N., Flanagan, O. and Güzeldere, G. (eds.) (1997). *The Nature of Consciousness: Philosophical and Scientific Debates.* Cambridge: MIT Press.

Broad, C. D. (1938). *An Examination of McTaggart's Philosophy.* Cambridge: Cambridge University Press.

Dainton, B. (2000). *Stream of Consciousness.* London: Routledge.

———. (2002). 'The Gaze of Consciousness'. *Journal of Consciousness Studies*, 9, No. 2, pp. 31–48.

———. (2003). 'Time in Experience: Reply to Gallagher'. *Psyche* 2003. http://psyche.cs.monash.edu.au/symposia/dainton/index.html

Epstein, R. (2000). 'The Neural-Cognitive Basis of the Jamesian Stream of Thought', *Consciousness and Cognition*, 9, 550–575.

Evans, C. O. (1970). *The Subject of Consciousness.* London: George Allen & Unwin Ltd. Online at: http://www.mentalstates.net/SOC.html

Foster, J. (1979). 'In *self*-defence' in G.F. Macdonald (ed.) *Perception and Identity*, London: Macmillan.

Husserl, E. (1991). *On the Phenomenology of the Consciousness of Internal Time (1893–1917)*, edited and translated by J. B. Brough. Dordrecht: Kluwer.

James, W. (1952). *The Principles of Psychology.* Chicago: Encyclopedia Britannica Inc.

Johnston, Mark. (1987). 'Human Beings,' *Journal of Philosophy* 84: 59–83.

Locke, J. (1959). *An Essay Concerning Human Nature*, Vol. 1. New York: Dover

Lockwood, M. (1989). *Mind, Brain and the Quantum.* Oxford: Blackwell.

Lycan, W. (1997). 'Consciousness as Internal Monitoring', in Block *et al.*

Mangan, B. (2001). 'Sensation's Ghost: The Non-Sensory "Fringe" of Consciousness' Psyche, 7(18), October 2001.

Nathan, N. M. L. (1997). 'Self and Will'. *International Journal of Philosophical Studies*, Vol. 5 (1), pp. 81–94.

Pöppel, E. (1985). *Mindworks: Time and Conscious Experience*, New York: Harcourt Brace Jovanovich

Robinson, H. (forthcoming). 'Personal identity, self and time', in A. Batthany (ed.) *Mind: its Place in the World. Non-reductionist Approaches to the Ontology of Consciousness*, Vienna.

Rosenthal, D. (1986). 'Two Conceptions of Consciousness', *Philosophical Studies*, 94: 3, pp. 329–359.

Russell, B. (1984). 'On the experience of time', in *The Collected Papers of Bertrand Russell Volume 7*, London: George Allen and Unwin.

---

[13] My thanks to Tim Bayne, Graham Nerlich and Galen Strawson for helpful comments and discussion.

Sprigge, T. (1983) *The Vindication of Absolute Idealism.* Edinburgh: Edinburgh University Press.

Strawson, G. (1999). 'The Self and the SESMET', *Journal of Consciousness Studies,* 6, No. 4, pp. 99–135.

Whitehead, A. N. (1929). *Process and Reality.* Cambridge: Cambridge University Press.

CHAPTER 2

SELF-DOUBT: WHY WE ARE NOT IDENTICAL
TO THINGS OF ANY KIND

Ingmar Persson

1. Introduction

We refer to ourselves by means of tokens of the first-person pronoun, in the case of English, 'I'. Although it is not entirely uncontroversial, I shall take it that, if anything is one's self, it is the referent of these uses of 'I'. There are at least two philosophical questions that can be asked about this self. First, when we employ 'I' to refer to ourselves, what are the properties of ourselves by means of which we attempt to pick ourselves out for purposes of reference? Second, what is the essence or identity of these putative selves of ours, i.e., the entities we attempt to pick out? For this essence need not be the properties which make it possible for us to be objects of first-person reference, since we can surely exist even when we are not the objects of such reference (e.g., in periods of unconsciousness).

In section 2, I start with the first question and try to unearth the conditions for being a self, or a referent of tokens of 'I'. Section 3 expounds the view that these conditions are designed to pick out one's body as given in proprioception, or as perceived from the inside. In section 4, I address the second question: taking as my point of departure the obvious truth that, in reality, this body is essentially a human organism, I argue that this organism does not in fact fulfil the conditions for being a self. So, we cannot be identical to our human organisms. But then, section 5 concludes, we seem not to be identical to things of any kind, since nothing of any other kind can take the place of these organisms by satisfying the conditions of being a self or referent of tokens of 'I' designed for these organisms.

2. Conditions of selfhood

Whatever else is necessarily true of a self, it is surely a *subject of experience* in the sense that it is something to which experiential states (and normally dispositional mental states, like desires) are attributable. It is plausible to think that experiential states, like perceiving and thinking, must have a subject – something doing the perceiving and thinking – just as much as they need an object – something being perceived and thought. If anything is to be a self, it must be such a subject. I call this *the owner aspect* of the notion of the self.

It is this aspect of the concept of the self that on a Humean 'bundle-theory' would have no persisting counterpart in reality.[1] A familiar difficulty besetting this theory is that if experiential states could not be attributed to any subjects, but were 'free-floating', how could we tell apart – what would be the difference between – two simultaneously occurring qualitatively identical experiences, having the same objects? It would be of no avail if these experiences were to interlock with other free-floating experiences to form 'bundles', for these bundles, too, could exist in duplicate. It would help, however, if experiences were not free-floating, but were ascribable to physical subjects that can be individuated by reference to their location in space,[2] and it will soon transpire how such subjects could emerge. Perhaps there is a way of construing a non-physical subject so that it could play this individuating role, but this is not something I undertake to do.

A second aspect of selfhood or being a self is that the self must in some way *be aware of itself*. In a world like ours, there would scarcely be subjects having or owning experiences, unless being equipped with these features had had survival value. The fact that animals are capable of perceiving their environment, prey and predators in the vicinity, increases their chances of survival. But it would not do so, unless they perceived *themselves*, i.e., the subjects possessing the relevant perceptions, in relation to surrounding objects. It would be of little use for the bird to perceive the stalking cat, unless it perceived the spatial relation in which the cat stands to *it itself*.

Let us call this aspect – that a self is necessarily capable of perceiving itself – *the phenomenal aspect* of the notion of the self. It concerns the self entering into the *content* of some of the states of (perceptual) experience that are attributable to it as their subject.

---

[1] *A Treatise of Human Nature* [1739–40], 2nd. rev. by P. H. Nidditch (Oxford: Clarendon Press, 1978), p. 252.
[2] A locus classicus for this line of thought is P. F. Strawson, *Individuals* (London: Methuen, 1959), chap. 3.

It is this aspect which Hume has in mind when he writes that there are philosophers 'who imagine we are every moment intimately conscious of what we call our SELF' (*A Treatise of Human Nature*, p. 251). He repudiates this aspect, when he affirms that 'there is no impression constant and invariable' (p. 251) as an impression of the self must be if the self is to persist through time. But, to repeat, if we had not in some way perceived ourselves in relation to an often hostile environment, we would not have lasted long.

It may be objected that, although this Darwin-inspired consideration shows that in *this* world conscious beings must have the capacity to perceive themselves, it does not show this to be a necessary truth, holding in every possible world. That is true, and I am willing to grant the possibility of 'self-blind' (or rather, as will be seen, 'self-numb') creatures. More specifically, I think there could conceivably be creatures who saw and heard things from mere 'points' which for them had no experiential content. Perhaps they could be said to be subjects of experience in virtue of conforming to the owner aspect, in virtue of there being something at these 'points' to which their experiences could be attributed (by others). But, I submit, they would not be, or have, *selves*.

This would not be just because they do not meet the phenomenal aspect, however. A bird, for instance, does that, and yet we hesitate to concede that it is, or has, a self. It is a subject of experience, though. Henceforth, 'subject of experience' will designate what meets both the owner and the phenomenal aspects, since in the present world 'pointillistic' subjects would be exceptional. A subject of, e.g., perceptual experience must then be an object of its own perceptions.

The reason why the bird is not a self is presumably that, though it perceives itself, e.g., as standing in spatial relations to surrounding objects, like the cat, and, as this implies, perceives itself as having spatial properties, like shape, size and position, and related properties, like colour, it is not aware of itself *as an owner of experiences*. That is to say, the bird does not attribute experiential states to itself: it does not think of itself as *seeing* the cat, as *thinking* that the cat is approaching, etc. We may call this aspect – which in my usage drives in a wedge between selves and subjects of experience – *the introspective aspect* of selves. Thus, a self must possess this third aspect, in addition to the two aspects definitive of subjects of experience.

I conjecture that the third, introspective aspect presupposes the second, phenomenal aspect, that it is by (correctly) taking this phenomenal aspect as presenting a *physical* thing – in the sense of a thing capable of existing (also) unperceived – that one acquires the notion of a subject to which one can ascribe one's experiential states. This implies that the phenomenal aspect is a necessary condition for introspection of one's experiential states (so even if there were pointillistic subjects, these could never be selves). But it is not the case that this perception of oneself *is* introspection (the bird does not introspect). We should keep apart perceiving oneself as a spatial *object* among other spatial objects and being aware of oneself as a *subject* that is in experiential states, like perceiving oneself in relation to other spatial objects. My proposal is that (correctly) taking the former self-perception, the phenomenal aspect, as veridical, as presenting a physical thing, is necessary for ascribing experiences to oneself, for being aware of oneself as a subject owning experiences, i.e., is necessary for introspective self-consciousness.[3]

Contrary to this, Sydney Shoemaker maintains that introspective 'self-awareness is not perceptual awareness, i.e., is not that sort of awareness in which objects are presented'.[4] In his opinion, this self-awareness 'is not mediated by anything analogous to a sense-impression [of ourselves]' ('A Materialist Account', p. 104). But those experiential states we are aware of ourselves as having in this self-awareness are attributed to *the very same entity* – viz. ourselves – as those spatial attributes we perceive ourselves as having. While Shoemaker's view does not yield an explanation of why this should be so, mine has the merit of yielding a very simple explanation of this circumstance.

According to the picture here sketched, one's self-consciousness begins with an ability to attribute, on the basis of perception, spatially related attributes to oneself, e.g., the ones needed to stand in certain spatial relations to something else. It then advances to conceptually registering one's experiential states, e.g., one's *perceiving* standing in these spatial relations. The progression is from having the perception-based thought, e.g., 'There is a cross in front of me' to thinking 'I see a cross (being) in front

---

[3]   For further elaboration of this proposal, see my 'Awareness of One's Body as Subject and Object', *Philosophical Explorations*, 2 (1999), pp. 70–6.

[4]   'A Materialist's Account' in Sydney Shoemaker & Richard Swinburne, *Personal Identity* (Oxford: Blackwell, 1984), p. 105.

of me'. These experiences are ascribed to oneself as a perceived spatial object or body. That is, one's body which has hitherto satisfied only the phenomenal aspect, takes on the introspective aspect, by one's conception of its phenomenal aspect as an owner of experiences.

I have also suggested that taking the phenomenal aspect to be physical is necessary for the conception of oneself as a subject of experiences. This raises issues I cannot explore here, but it sits well with the observation that mental states can be individuated only if they are moored in physical space, that there cannot be in this sense individual, free-floating mental states. (But since the notion of a physical object has been explained in terms of existence independent of perception, the concept of the physical seems to involve the concept of something mental. If so, there would be an inter-dependency between the mental and the physical, but this is a corollary I need not pursue here.)

A self, then, is something that (1) owns or has experiences (not to mention other mental states of a propositional and dispositional kind, like beliefs and desires), that (2) perceives itself, or enters into the content of some of its experiential states, and that (3) is aware of itself as something of which (1) is true. The introspective aspect, (3), involves taking the phenomenal aspect, (2), to be of something physical, in the sense of existing independently of perception. Introspective self-consciousness (3) entails, I have urged, objective self-consciousness (2).

My starting point in section 1 was that, if the self is anything, it is that to which we refer by means of 'I'. I cannot think of any less question-begging way of fixing what is the object of an investigation into 'the self' than this.[5] Now, let us see how the account of the self given by (1)–(3) plugs into this starting point. It is a commonplace that, just as, e.g., the use of 'now' is governed by the rule that a token of it refers to the time at which it is produced, so the use of 'I' is governed by the rule that a token of it refers to the producer of it. This producer, as construed by (2), is a perceived spatial object, one's own body as perceived by oneself. Thus, to consciously follow the rule is to use a token of 'I' to refer to the perceived body which is the subject or owner of the mental property of producing this token of 'I' in awareness of the rule.

---

[5] The importance of fixing precisely what the topic is when one discusses 'the self' is made clear by Eric T. Olson, 'There is no Problem of the Self', *Journal of Consciousness Studies*, 6 (1999), pp. 49–61.

This self-reference consequently involves the ascription of mental properties definitive of introspection.

3. The self and proprioception

I want now to examine more closely how we perceive our own bodies. Michael Ayers maintains that we have 'bodily sensations of ourselves as objects extended in space'.[6] The objects we tactually feel are also felt to be extended in (three-dimensional) space, but, I submit, every one of us perceives their own body, and only their own body, differently. Although what we tactually feel may present itself as three-dimensional when, e.g., we hold a ball in the palm of our hand, what we feel as three-dimensionally extended are two-dimensional *surfaces*: we do not feel the ball as *filling* the space enclosed by its surface (though from its felt weight we guess that it is not hollow). In contrast, we are proprioceptively aware of the *mass* of our own bodies as *filling three-dimensional* regions of space; we are aware of them as three-dimensional *solids*, of a rough human body like shape.[7] This is the source of our notion of solidity and, thus, of a three-dimensional thing or body as something having this property.

Visual space is three-dimensional, too, but it is perceived as stretching out from a *single* point of view. In contrast, the felt three-dimensional solidity of our bodies is constituted by sensations from innumerable 'points of feeling' spread out in three-dimensional space, i.e., from receptors spread out through the interior of our bodies. Neither vision nor tactile perception nor any other mode of perception of the external world can produce the unique impression of 3-D solidity or of filling through and through a (3-D) region of space.

It is because one's proprioceptive or somatosensory awareness is an awareness not just of surfaces, but of this 3-D solidity, that

---

[6] See *Locke* (London & New York: Routledge, 1991), vol. II, p. 285.

[7] Cf. Ingmar Persson, *The Primacy of Perception* (Lund: Gleerups, 1985), chap. 4.5. For an elaborate analysis of bodily awareness, see Brian O'Shaughnessy, *The Will* (Cambridge: Cambridge University Press, 1980), vol. I, chaps. 6 & 7 and 'Proprioception and the Body Image' in J. L. Bermúdez, A. Marcel & N. Eilan, eds., *The Body and the Self* (Cambridge, MA: MIT Press, 1995). But, contrary to my inclinations, O'Shaughnessy in his book views bodily awareness as disanalogous to perception and as not presenting 'an existent experienced entity' (p. 230). In contrast, J. L. Bermúdez argues that proprioception is perception of oneself in *The Paradox of Self-Consciousness* (Cambridge, MA: MIT Press, 1998), chap. 6.

one can feel bodily sensations – like pains and pangs of hunger – *inside* one's body, somewhere in-between where one feels, e.g., a pressure on one's back and an itch around one's navel. A disturbance or damage occurring practically anywhere inside our bodies may cause us pain or some other sort of unpleasant bodily sensation in that region.

Ayers further claims that this proprioceptive awareness of our own body 'essentially permeates our sensory experience of things in general' or is 'integrated with the deliverances of each of the senses' (*Locke*, vol. II, p. 285). Thus, one sees and hears things in relation to one's proprioceptive presentation of one's head, has tactile sensations on the surfaces of proprioceptive presentations of limbs in touch with objects, gustatory sensations in proprioceptive presentations of the mouth and olfactory ones in the neighbourhood of proprioceptive presentations of the nostrils and palate. This 'proprioceptive "body model"', as Ayers terms it (*Locke*, vol. I, p. 187), is the common denominator of what we perceive in all our sense-modalities: it is normally present whenever we perceive and are conscious of anything.[8] Therefore, it provides us with a centre around which we can spatially organize all our perceptual presentations of external objects, and on the surface of which or within which we can locate our bodily sensations. Moreover, its parts are involved in our kinesthetic sensations.

My claim is that this felt three-dimensional 'model' of our bodies, the centre-piece of our perceptual or phenomenal world, taken as presenting a real, physical thing, constitutes the subject to which we ordinarily attribute our perceptual and other mental states. If correct, this account of the subject of experience has the merit of undercutting scepticism about the physical world. As we have seen, the notion of an experiential state, e.g., the state of perceiving something, logically requires a subject. Now, *if* this subject can be conceived only by taking something in the perceptual content to be a physical thing, a general doubt about whether this content presents anything of physical reality would of course be ruled out. For asking whether a perceptual content presents something physical, i.e., something that exists inde-

---

[8]   There are aberrations; for an instance, consult Oliver Sacks's story of 'the disembodied lady' in *The Man Who Mistook His Wife For a Hat* (New York: Summit Books, 1985), chap. 3. This unfortunate woman has a conception of herself, I surmise, only because she earlier perceived her body from the inside.

pendently of the perceiving of it, requires a concept of the perceptual state of which it is the content, and this in turn requires a notion of a subject obtained by taking something in the content to be a physical thing. Therefore, a general scepticism about whether perceptual content presents physical reality would be undercut (though this is not a point I need for present purposes).

Perhaps some would like to object to this identification of subject of experience and body that it is strange to say that our *bodies* perceive and think.[9] I believe this is like objecting 'It is not *men* but *policemen* who enforce the law'. The reason why it sounds odd to say that *bodies* perceive and think is, I conjecture, that if something is described as a 'body', it is 'conversationally implied' that it is a *mere* body, shorn of any mental capacities, just as if law-enforcers are described as 'men', it is implied that they are mere men, lacking the relevant authority. Moreover, note that it is not in the least awkward to say that *organisms* perceive and think but, surely, organisms *are* bodies (with a life-sustaining constitution, I will contend in the next section).

Galen Strawson raises the different objection that one can

> well imagine a three-bodied creature that naturally experiences itself as three-bodied, and as receiving information (perhaps via different sense modalities) from all three bodies, while still having a strong sense of the single mental self, and thinking of itself as 'I'.[10]

So, although Strawson is prepared to concede that 'ordinary human experience of oneself as a mentally single is deeply shaped by experience of having a single body', he denies that 'any possible experience of oneself as a mentally single depends essentially on such experience' ('"The Self"', p. 414).

I think the 'three-bodied' situation Strawson envisages must be further specified for it to become clear what, if any, challenge it presents to the view here proposed. Let me just say with respect to the proprioceptive awareness of our body as a 3-D solid, which according to my view constitutes the core of the phenomenal aspect of the self, that I cannot see how anyone could have such an awareness of three bodies that presents them *as separate*, i.e.,

---

[9]   E.g., E. J. Lowe, *Subjects of Experience* (Cambridge: Cambridge University Press, 1996), p. 1.

[10]   '"The Self"', *Journal of Consciousness Studies*, 4 (1997), pp. 405–28, p. 414.

as separated by empty space. For this is an awareness of something (offering felt resistance) *filling* a three-dimensional region. Such an awareness cannot represent the empty space between distinct bodies. So, if one had proprioceptive awareness of three distinct bodies, they would have to be experienced as adjoining each other and so forming a unity. (I am unsure, however, how this unity relates to Strawson's 'experience of oneself as mentally single' which 'is deeply shaped by experience of having a single body'.)

4. Two doubts about the identity of ourselves and our organisms

If it is our bodies that satisfy the conditions of selfhood, (1)–(3) – i.e., that are the perceived objects that we rightly recognize to be the owners of our mental lives – then we are identical to these bodies if we are identical to any kind of thing. It follows from this identification of us with our bodies that we are not *essentially* selves, i.e., it is not necessarily true that, whenever we exist, we are selves.[11] For (1)–(3) are not essential properties of our bodies: plainly, our bodies existed (prenatally) before acquiring these properties and may persist after losing them (in a state of permanent unconsciousness). Being selves is just a 'phase' we pass through, like being adults. Nothing psychological is necessary for our existence. This is concordant with the fact that we are quite ready to say things like 'If I were ever to sink into a permanently vegetative state, I want you to kill *me*' or 'My mother thought of aborting *me* in the twelfth week'. Both of these statements presuppose that I can exist without being a self.

What would wreak havoc on the identification of us with our bodies, however, is the reverse possibility: if whatever it is about us that makes us selves could persist while our bodies pass away. For this implies that we cannot be identical to our bodies – and that our bodies are only something that in ordinary circumstances coincides with what fulfils the conditions of selfhood; since our selves cannot outlive us. I shall now look at two cases which in different ways show that we cannot be identical to our bodies. Only

---

[11] Contrast, e.g., Robert Nozick's claim 'that selves are essentially selves, that anything which is a self could not have existed yet been otherwise', *Philosophical Explanations* (Oxford: Clarendon Press, 1981), p. 79.

the second case shows that we can persist in the absence of our bodies. It is commonly thought that the first case also shows this, but in fact it shows only that the owner of our experiences is, strictly, not our whole bodies, but only proper parts of them and so that *this* aspect of the self, the owner aspect, does not require our whole bodies to persist.

Is the Body Really the Owner of Our Experiences? Strictly speaking, it seems that it is not the *whole* human body that is the owner of experiences. The owner is rather its brain, or even certain parts of the brain, for these are what is *minimally sufficient* for the occurrence of the experiences. It is nomologically possible that a stream of experiences continues, even though almost all of a human body is annihilated, as long as certain cerebral parts are kept alive in certain states. The fact that the body possesses experiences is therefore *derivative* from their being possessed by proper parts of it: the body has experiences *in virtue of* having certain proper parts that *primarily* have them (i.e., that have them, but not in virtue of having any proper part that in turn has them).[12]

So construed, the practice of attributing experiential properties to human bodies is of a piece with an exceedingly common pattern. We observe that something exercises some power, e.g., that a liquid or a gas poisons or intoxicates us. Only later do we discover that it does so in virtue of containing a certain chemical, that is, that the applicability of these predicates to it is derivative from the applicability of them to the chemical. Similarly, we observe that our bodies have experiences. It is only later that we establish that they have these experiences in virtue of having certain organs, that is, that the applicability of these experiential predicates to them is derivative from the applicability of (a core of) them to these parts.

---

[12] This idea is further developed in my paper 'Our Identity and the Separability of Persons and Organisms', *Dialogue*, 38 (1999), pp. 519–33. In contrast, Lynne Rudder Baker so defines the distinction between derivative and non-derivative attribution that only persons have person-making properties non-derivatively, whereas their organisms and their parts have them only derivatively; see *Persons and Bodies* (Cambridge: Cambridge University Press, 2000), e.g., pp. 97–8). However, Baker's view has a counter-intuitive implication, noted by her (pp. 101–5): since their organisms will non-derivatively have simpler mental properties, like feeling physical pain, these will non-derivatively belong to another subject than the person-making properties. Consequently, when I am introspectively aware of a pain I am feeling, I am aware of a pain that is really felt by a subject distinct from me doing the introspecting.

Doesn't my claim that experiential properties are first attributed to our whole bodies conflict with the claim that their possession of these properties is derivative? No, it is in an *epistemic*
sense that the attribution of these properties to whole bodies is
prior. This is consistent with this attribution being *ontically* derivative, while the attribution of these properties to proper parts of
our bodies is ontically non-derivative or primary. My claim is that
for something to satisfy the owner aspect, the attribution of experiences to it must be non-derivative in the ontic sense.

Does this mean that it is not a human body, but rather certain
parts of it and its brain, that are the subject of experience and the
self? No, for although (a part of) the brain matches the owner
aspect, is the primary or non-derivative mind-owner, it does not
match the phenomenal aspect. For a brain does not perceive itself
and would therefore be unable to ascribe the experiences it owns
to itself, i.e., it could not be conscious of itself as a subject (having
mental properties) because it is not conscious of itself as an object
(having material properties).

The pull of the phenomenal aspect is felt if we imagine, as in
Daniel Dennett's well-known thought-experiment,[13] that my brain
is taken out of my body and kept alive in a vat distant from my
brainless body. By radio transmission my brain receives impulses
from this body, so there is still proprioception of it and exteroception by means of its sense-organs. Here we are torn between
saying that I am where my brain is and that I am where my body
is. This conundrum is due, I hypothesize, to the fact that what
carries the owner aspect is rather the brain, while the rest of my
body aspires to carry the phenomenal aspect. The source of the
conundrum is not simply that my body is 'scattered', by one part
of it being distant from the rest,[14] for there would be no conundrum if, say, it was instead my bowels that had this location; the
isolated part has to be the owner of my mind. Nor would there
be a conundrum if there were not also a tendency to identify
oneself with the phenomenal aspect, with the body as perceived
from the inside.

Given the latter tendency, what explains the common feeling
that in imagined cases of transplant we follow our brains (or whatever piece of matter is minimally sufficient for our minds)? The

---

[13] See 'Where Am I?' in his *Brainstorms* (Montgomery, VT: Bradford Books, 1978).
[14] *Pace* Brian Garrett, *Personal Identity and Self-Consciousness* (London: Routledge, 1998),
p. 47.

explanation presumably has to do with the rough coincidence in space between the owner and phenomenal aspects – because the brain is inside the body perceived – causing a failure to separate them and to realize that identity in each aspect is necessary for our identity. So, it is overlooked that identity in the phenomenal aspect is a necessary condition for our identity. This condition is obviously not met in transplant cases because after the operation a numerically distinct body is playing the phenomenal role.

If the conviction that we go with our brains in transplant cases were right, we would need an explanation of why we do not unequivocally hold that in Dennett's case our location is that of the brain in the vat. Moreover, what would explain the fact, noted in the beginning of this section, that we are inclined to hold that we can persist in a state of being permanently unconscious? This may be the state of the donor body after the removal of its higher cerebral parts, which are the owner of experiences, and we cannot identify ourselves both with the transplanted brain-parts and with the living body left behind.[15]

My hypothesis is, then, that we unequivocally identify ourselves only with that which meets *both* the owner and the phenomenal aspect of the concept of self. In our commonsensical moments, we assume that our bodies meet this double requirement. Brain-transplant cases reveal that one part of this assumption is false: these bodies do not really meet the owner aspect, since our experiences are only derivatively attributable to them. This suffices for brain-transplant cases to show that we cannot be identical to our bodies. But these cases do not show, as is often thought, that we can outlive our bodies by going with our brains, for our brains satisfy only the owner aspect, not the phenomenal aspect. I now turn to another case that amplifies the doubt about the tenability of the identification of us with our bodies precisely by showing how we can outlast them, by the persistence of something that satisfies both aspects.

Does the Organism Really Answer to the Phenomenal Aspect? Consider now a thought-experiment which shows that there can be identity as regards the phenomenal aspect – and, thereby, as regards that to which we (epistemically) first attribute our expe-

---

[15]   The identification of ourselves with that which merely owns our minds is fraught with further difficulties that I cannot here explore. For an argument against certain forms of this identification, see my 'The Involvement of Our Identity in Experiential Memory', *Canadian Journal of Philosophy*, 27, 4 (1997), pp. 447–65.

riences – without identity of human body. It turns on the fact that the human body is an *organism* belonging to a certain *biological species*, *homo sapiens*, and that the nature or essence of such an entity is not open to the view of its consciousness, so that a human organism can cease to exist without this showing up in the phenomenal aspect, in what is given to the organism in proprioception (or in exteroception for that matter). Thus, there can conceivably be identity as regards this aspect, which is logically sufficient for the ascription of experiences to a subject (making up the owner aspect), without identity of human organism. If so, identity of human organism is not necessary for identity of that which is a self and, consequently, not for our identity, since the existence of that which makes us selves is surely sufficient for our existence.

What is the nature of (biological) organisms? There is clearly some connection between the concept of an organism and that of *biological life*, though it would seem that this connection is not so straightforward that we can say that something is an organism if and only if it is biologically alive (for 'dead organism' does not appear to be a *contradictio in adjecto*). This (vague) proposal however leaves us with another notoriously controversial issue: what is it to be biologically alive? One plausible suggestion would seem to be that to be alive consists in having a metabolism, in acquiring materials from the environment – by eating, drinking and breathing – and making them part of one's own body. It is this absorption of alien material that underlies the growth and development characteristic of living organisms.

According to this admittedly very sketchy account, the life-processes – and, hence, the organic status – of our bodies are not accessible to everyday observation. For although we observe that we breathe, eat, drink and excrete some products, we do not observe that our bodies absorb material from what we consume. As far as everyday perceptual awareness of ourselves goes, what we consume might just have supplied us with the energy needed to fuel our mental and outward bodily activities – or, indeed, it might have had no causal effect at all on us. This awareness is compatible with our having been inorganic, cleverly constructed robots with consciousnesses rather than living organisms. That is, everyday observation does not reveal our bodies to have a constitution that enables them to absorb alien material in the way characteristic of living organisms. Rather than presenting our bodies as organic, as organisms, proprioception and other forms of perception present them as mere bodies, i.e., as something tangible occupying three-dimensional spatial regions.

For present purposes, it is this obvious point about the organic nature of a body not lying in plain view, and not any more specific details of the analysis of the concepts of an organism and of its life, that is crucial. Note that a corresponding point can be made about what it is to be member of a biological species, like *homo sapiens*: this is surely a matter not only of morphological features observable 'in the field', but also of genetic properties unobservable in the course of everyday life. Consequently, the argument against the thesis that we are identical to organisms that I am about to set in motion can be adapted to tell against the thesis that we essentially belong to the human species.

Imagine that there were some inorganic material that had the power to sustain minds and behaviour like ours and that was supplied with energy by the substances we consume. If the organic material of our bodies bit by bit were transformed into this material, the resulting bodies would be subjects whose experiences could be 'seamlessly' continuous with our experiences.[16] As our proprioceptive and perceptual systems are unable to monitor life processes inside our bodies, we would not perceive any of the changes going on, and externally, our bodies would look and behave in the same manner. Now, if we were informed of these changes going on below the observable surface, we would hardly be inclined to exclaim 'Help, I am about to disappear!'. For, as we have seen, the first-person pronoun refers to the perceptually (mainly proprioceptively) given aspects of the physical body producing the current tokens of it, and there is identity in these aspects, though the organism is about to vanish. Therefore, a self cannot in this way be swept away by an undertow so to speak, while the stream of consciousness flows on.

This goes to show that to answer to the phenomenal aspect of the self, it is not enough that a physical thing is perceived. Rather, it must be 'transparent' to perception to the extent that it cannot pass out of existence without this being perceived. The thought-experiment demonstrates that because our bodies are essentially organisms (belonging to the species *homo sapiens*) they are not 'transparent' to us, as selves need to be,[17] according to the phe-

---

[16] Recently, Baker has also remarked upon the possibility of such a 'gradual replacement of organic by inorganic parts' (*Persons and Bodies*, p. 11; cf. p. 106).

nomenal aspect. Our organisms are given to us in proprioception as mere three-dimensional things and in exteroception as having the superficial, morphological features of humans. As long as there really is identity in these respects, as long as there really is something, having these features, continuously filling the relevant three-dimensional regions, there is identity in the phenomenal aspect. (Analogously, it may be said that 'a view' picks out certain visible aspects of, e.g., a landscape, and there is numerically the same view as long as these visible surfaces remain the same, even if there is not identity in respect of the material things having these surfaces.)

However, it might be questioned whether the self is really preserved in the thought-experiment on the different ground that it is doubtful whether the owner aspect of the self is preserved. For although the phenomenal aspect is preserved, and this is the epistemically primary subject of our experiential states, the ontically non-derivative owner is rather, as we have seen, (some part of) the brain, and the brain hardly persists if its body ceases to be organic. But, strictly speaking, the non-derivative owner of consciousness is not (a certain part of) the brain, but *whatever* fills the function that the (relevant part of the) brain now fills. Certainly it seems plausible to hold that the same consciousness or mind can survive the piecemeal replacement of minute parts of its brain by inorganic components having the same function.[18] In contrast, replacements at one go of the whole, or major parts, of a brain will put an end to numerically the same consciousness, however swiftly these replacements occur. But we can take it that the organic-inorganic metamorphosis envisaged proceeds gradually and at such a slow rate that identity of mind is not disrupted. This entails that the mind-owner is the same, since this is trivially so whenever there is sameness of mind (given that a mind must have a – physical – owner, as argued in section 2).

---

[17]   This is how Roderick Chisholm describes the self. He continues: 'to know that I perceive the cat to be standing, I must know that I perceive a proper part of the cat . . . but to know that I perceive myself to be thinking I need *not* know that I perceive a proper part of myself', 'On the Observability of the Self' in Quassim Cassam, ed., *Self-Knowledge* (Oxford: Oxford University Press, 1994), p. 100. That is, I need not know that my body has other, possibly essential, parts. This is why, in order to know whether I perceive the same cat, I must know what happens to parts of the cat that are not currently visible to me, but to know whether I go on existing, I need not know anything about unperceived parts of my body: it is enough if the perceived parts and the consciousness attributed to them go on existing.

[18]   Cf. Garrett, *Personal Identity and Self-Consciousness*, pp. 49–50.

So, to conclude, there is identity of subject of experience and self in the organic-inorganic transition, since it disrupts neither the phenomenal nor the owner aspect. As our (human) organisms do not survive this transition, it follows that our selves, i.e., the referents of our uses of 'I', cannot be identical to these organisms.

Underlying this argument is the assumption that we can identify ourselves by means of 'I' without knowing or fully understanding what kind of thing the thing intended to be picked out *essentially* is (a human organism). We pick out ourselves by means of features revealed in everyday perception, in particular proprioception. In this respect, first-person reference is similar to demonstrative reference: in both cases, it is enough that one is able to perceptually single out the thing intended from its environment.[19] For instance, to demonstratively refer to 'that worm-like thing' I perceive, I certainly do not need to know its kind and conditions of persistence, e.g., whether they allow its transforming into a butterfly. This is something that science may establish later. It suffices that I am able to perceptually tell it apart from its environment. The same is true of the producer of a current token of 'I' which stands out from the environment by being the only object proprioceptively given as a thing filling a 3-D region.

But there is a crucial difference between these cases. Suppose that I am informed that, underneath the qualitative continuity I perceive, the 'worm-like thing' undergoes a radical change from an organic to an inorganic state; then I will have to retract the identity-judgement that I am spontaneously inclined to make, to the effect that I perceive one and the same thing. For, with my current knowledge, I cannot specify any sort of thing which can undergo such changes without losing its identity. In contrast, I have argued that we need not retract our judgements that we, or our selves, persist in the same circumstances. We need not retract these judgements as long as there is identity in the phenomenal and owner aspects forming the core of the concept of the self. The self has a transparency which obstructs its being identical to something of a natural kind whose essence is hidden from the consciousness selves necessarily possess.

The organic-inorganic metamorphosis envisaged would however have been ruled out had it been true that the life of our

---

[19] Cf. Quassim Cassam, *Self and World* (Oxford: Clarendon Press, 1997), pp. 136 ff.

organisms is what 'holds them together', so that they would necessarily dissolve or disintegrate, even in observable respects, as
soon as they lost life. Along similar lines Peter van Inwagen maintains (i) that there is something that simples, the elementary particles of physics, compose if and only if their activity constitutes a
life,[20] and (ii) that if there is thinking and feeling 'there must
be a thing, one thing, that is doing the thinking and feeling'
(*Material Beings*, p. 12; cf. also sec. 12). It follows that non-living
collections of simples cannot think or feel. But van Inwagen
cannot plausibly mean that when an organism dies, it falls apart
in the sense that, to our sense experience, it no longer presents
itself as a unitary thing, for evidently a dead organism may to our
senses be indistinguishable from a living one.[21] It is then conceivable that a phenomenal unity and an attached stream of 'I'-
thoughts carry on, though the life-processes that pumped them
peter out.

The organic-inorganic transition would also be excluded if it
could be shown to be a necessary truth for some other reason that
only organisms can have minds. If the organic-inorganic transition inevitably extinguished the mind, the physical thing under-
going it could of course not present itself as unchanged to this
mind. But the crux is that this mind-life correlation has all the
appearance of being a *contingent* truth – for surely it is not *conceptually* impossible that inorganic things, e.g., computers, have
minds – if indeed it is a truth at all.

5. Conclusion: we are not identical to things of any kind

Our selves must logically be that to which our experiences are
non-derivatively attributable – the owner aspect – and the perception of ourselves that is necessary for the attribution of experiences to ourselves must be full in the sense of revealing the
essence of what is perceived – the phenomenal aspect. Prior to
philosophical reflection, we assume these demands to be satisfied
by our bodies. The two arguments in section 4 reveal, however,
that, our bodies in fact fulfil neither the owner aspect nor the
phenomenal aspect: our bodies are neither *non-derivatively*

---

[20] *Material Beings* (Ithaca & London: Cornell University Press, 1990), sec. 9.
[21] For further discussion of van Inwagen's book, see my 'Critical Study', *Noûs* 27, 4
(1993), pp. 512–8.

the owners of our experiences, nor are they *transparent* to us in the sense that their essence is perceived. Our ordinary use of 'I' to refer to ourselves assumes that this reference is to our bodies because, I suggest, it overlooks the fact that our bodies are only the derivative owners of our experiences and that they are non-transparent or opaque. These oversights are understandable for, first, in everyday life derivative and non-derivative ownership do not clearly come apart, e.g., by brains being kept alive outside our bodies.[22] Secondly, the opacity of our bodies is not displayed by our human organisms ceasing to exist while the aspects of them given in proprioception and exteroception continue unchanged. But as soon as these oversights are rectified, it becomes apparent that our selves cannot *be* our human organisms.

Now, there can scarcely be any other kind of material thing to which that which satisfies the owner and the phenomenal aspects of the notion of the self essentially belongs. As material things of a certain shape, our organisms satisfy the phenomenal aspect, but this evidently provides no specification of any kind of thing with distinctive conditions of identity. Besides, it is our brains – or, strictly, some processes in them which in principle are transferable to something inorganic – that satisfy the owner aspect, but they plainly fail to satisfy the phenomenal aspect. Clearly the things that satisfy each of these two aspects do not together form any kind of thing, as would have been the case if both had been satisfied by our human organisms. These 'satisfiers' are lumped together only because of their relation to something else, our mind or mental states. So, as used by us, tokens of 'I' do not identify things of any kind that can take the place of our human organisms. But, if so, we are not identical to things of any kind, i.e., there is no philosophically defensible criterion of our persistence.

This conclusion may seem absurd for, if we are not identical to things of any kind, it would seem we do not exist! But even though tokens of 'I' do not correctly identify the material things they are supposed to identify, our human organisms, there are different parts of these organisms making different bits of this identification true: we do perceive something of these organisms and something (else) of them owns our experiences. Therefore, these

---

[22] Certain rare cases of conjoined or Siamese twins also present a difficulty. For further discussion, see my 'Our Identity and the Separability of Persons and Organisms', pp. 525–7.

tokens have enough of reference for us to exist. But what is identified by them does not belong to any kind of thing with its own
conditions of identity. Hence, we exist, but are not identical to
things forming any kind.[23]

[23] I am grateful to E. J. Lowe, Ray Martin, Eric Olson, Derek Parfit, Paul Snowdon,
Galen Strawson and to participants in the *Ratio* conference for many valuable comments.

CHAPTER 3

SELF-EXPRESSION AND SELF-CONTROL

Marya Schechtman

It is a commonplace that people are sometimes 'not themselves.' Frequently this is said to happen when the usual mechanisms of self-control are compromised – when someone is drunk for instance, or under a great deal of stress. Strangely enough, these are precisely the circumstances under which it is also often said that people are 'most fully themselves' or 'reveal their true natures.' This presents a *prima facie* puzzle about how we are to understand the relation between these two truisms. This puzzle becomes more compelling in the context of philosophical work which takes the sentiments expressed in them literally, suggesting that a person can genuinely fail to be herself.

In what follows, I consider the relation between these two pronouncements about when a person might fail to be herself. Each, I argue, expresses a picture of the self which can be found in the philosophical literature. I use the work of Harry Frankfurt to represent the first picture – that being oneself requires self-control. I examine the second picture – that being oneself involves expressing one's nature – as it occurs in a common objection to Frankfurt. Considering Frankfurt's work and the objection to it, we get clearer on the two pictures of the self at issue and where they oppose one another. These approaches capture two distinct and independent senses of what we call 'self'. I claim, however, that they are also connected by the link they draw between being a self and living a life one finds meaningful. This connection points to an integrated picture of the self which has somewhat broader applicability.

I

Having or being a self is often considered to be an achievement typical of fully functioning adult humans. To define the self we

may thus focus on the unique,[1] defining features of human existence. Harry Frankfurt's approach can be read this way. In his
picture, the relevant distinguishing feature of human life is found
in the structure of the will. An early statement of this view is found
in 'Freedom of the Will and the Concept of the Person' where he
tells us that 'human beings are not alone in having desires and
motives, or in making choices.' What is special to human beings,
he says, is that 'besides wanting and choosing and being moved
to do this or that, men may also want to have (or not to have)
certain desires and motives. They are capable of wanting to be different, in their preferences and purposes, from what they are.'[2]
The defining feature of selfhood is thus the ability to take sides
when we discover conflicts in our desires, rather than simply
being moved by whichever desire is on-balance strongest. It is this
capacity, Frankfurt says, that allows for the type of autonomy
which defines human action, and so it is in virtue of this capacity
that we are *selves*.

This analysis of self implies that not all of the desires a person
experiences will be internal to her *self*. Roughly put, those with
which she sides will be part of her self, while those she repudiates, though part of her psychological history, are in the relevant
sense external. Certain phenomena familiar from everyday life,
can help to clarify this basic idea and underscore its plausibility.
Addiction is one such phenomenon, and one of Frankfurt's most
frequently invoked examples is that of the unwilling addict. An
addict might repudiate her addictive desires, struggling against
them with all of her strength. Despite this, these desires may prove
too powerful, and she may relapse. In such a case she is in a very
real sense acting against her own wishes. When this happens, says
Frankfurt, the motivation which leads her to action is external to
her*self* – it is not *she* who is acting, but the addiction which acts
through her.

The crux of this view is obviously the notion of 'taking sides',
which Frankfurt calls 'identification.' To make the view work it is
essential to offer a viable account of what it is to identify with a
desire in the relevant sense. As a first approximation, identifica-

---

[1]   At least so far as we know. Humans are taken to be the paradigm cases of selves, and
so selfhood is defined in terms of what seems characteristic of them. None of the figures
we will be discussing rules out a priori that other creatures might turn out to have those
same features, and so be selves.

[2]   Harry Frankfurt, 'Freedom of the Will and the Concept of a Person', in *The Importance of What We Care About* (Cambridge: Cambridge University Press, 1988), p. 12.

tion can be viewed as a higher-order endorsement of a first-order desire. The unwilling addict experiences both a first-order desire to indulge her addiction, and a first-order desire to resist it. In addition, however, she experiences a second-order desire to be moved to action by the desire for resistance rather than the desire for indulgence, and in this sense she identifies with the one desire and repudiates the other. While this captures the basic idea behind identity-constituting identification and repudiation, it cannot be the entire story. For one thing, an account of internality based purely on higher-order attitudes is faced with a serious regress problem. Second-order desires can also be in conflict, and if these conflicts must be resolved by appeal to yet higher-order desires – which of course can also be in conflict – the possibility of regress looms large.

To address this problem, Frankfurt argues that self-constituting identification must be 'wholehearted'. He gives two different accounts of wholeheartedness. The first gives a prominent role to *decision*. In 'Identification and Wholeheartedness,' he tells us that 'it is characteristically by a decision (though, of course, not necessarily or even most frequently in that way) that a sequence of desires or preferences of increasingly higher orders is terminated. When the decision is made without reservation, the commitment it entails is decisive.'[3] A decision, he says, represents a commitment to one motivating desire or passion over another in a way that cuts off appeal to higher-order desires. 'When the decision is made without reservation, the commitment it entails is decisive. Then the person no longer holds himself apart from the desire to which he has committed himself. It is no longer unsettled or uncertain whether the object of that desire – that is, what he wants – is what he really wants.' He goes on to say that 'to this extent, the person, in making a decision by which he identifies with a desire, *constitutes himself*.'[4]

Later, in 'The Faintest Passion', Frankfurt presents a picture of wholeheartedness which is independent of decision. Here wholehearted commitment is defined in terms of satisfaction – a certain stability in the structure of one's higher-order attitudes. 'To be satisfied with something does not require that a person have any particular belief about it, nor any particular feeling or attitude or

[3]   Harry Frankfurt, 'Identification and Wholeheartedness', in *The Importance of What We Care About*, p. 170.
[4]   ibid.

intention. It does not require, for instance, that he regard it as satisfactory, or that he accede to it with approval, or that he intend to leave it as it stands.'[5] To be satisfied is rather to have a certain equilibrium in one's higher-order attitudes which leaves one 'simply *having no interest*' in making changes.'[6] It is not, in this case a *decision* or any other psychological act which seals identification, but rather a fact about the structure of the will.

On either account of wholeheartedness, however, the basic picture is the same. What is required to identify with – or repudiate – a desire, is to achieve a certain sort of stability or equilibrium with respect to one's attitude towards it. This is not a stability which implies a lack of conflict – Frankfurt repeats many times that wholehearted repudiation of a desire will not necessarily make it disappear, and attempts to resist it may cause a great deal of psychic distress. What is settled, however, is that no matter how powerful the repudiated desire, it is not taken as a legitimate candidate for satisfaction. Its persistence does not lead the person to rethink her commitment to struggling against it.

It is also important to realize that on either account, although wholeheartedness is a feature of the will, the fact of wholeheartedness is rarely under our immediate control. We cannot wholeheartedly identify with any desire we choose. The capacity for wholeheartedness will usually be determined by a host of contingent factors about one's constitution and history. Nonetheless, since the self is *created* through the formation of a unified will, once we *are* wholeheartedly behind a desire, however we came to be so, it simply *is*, in virtue of that wholeheartedness, the desire that represents what *we* (*as* selves) most want to do.

Here, then, is Frankfurt's basic picture: We start, like other animals, with a collection of desires, motivations, and passions, some of which are stronger and more salient than others, some of which are in conflict, and some of which are not. This leads to natural orderings and resolutions which result from a more-or-less mechanical interaction between desires of different forces. In addition, however, we have another dimension of evaluation and resolution – 'it is a salient characteristic of human beings, one which affects our lives in deep and innumerable ways, that we care

[5]   Harry Frankfurt, 'The Faintest Passion,' in *Necessity, Volition, and Love* (Cambridge: Cambridge University Press, 1999), p. 104.
[6]   Frankfurt, 'The Faintest Passion', p. 105.

about what we are'.[7] Because we care about what we are, we form attitudes towards the desires and motivations we experience. In many cases we may be ambivalent or unsettled, but at least sometimes we find that we either wholeheartedly embrace or repudiate a desire. When this happens, we create a distinction between what *we* want, and desires and motivations which merely occur in our psychological history, but are not ours. In this way, a self is created out of the 'raw materials of inner life'.[8]

We can now see more clearly how Frankfurt's view can serve as a representative of the picture of self behind the truism that a person may be 'not himself' when his self-control is compromised. On the view we have laid out here, a person is 'not himself' when, e.g., despite his wholehearted repudiation of a desire it proves too powerful to resist, and he acts on it. Insofar as conditions of drunkenness, stress, fatigue or illness compromise the resources we have with which to battle outlaw desires, they make it more likely that we will act upon them, and so fail to be ourselves.

II

While Frankfurt's view captures our sense that being ourselves requires self-control, it seems open to challenges based on the fact that we frequently view overly rigid self-control as an impediment to being oneself. This is the idea expressed in the second truism mentioned in the introduction – that people are often most truly themselves when inhibition fails. Whatever the picture of the self standing behind this truism, it obviously cannot define the self in terms of identification and self-control. On this picture the self resides in repudiated desires which break through despite a person's struggles against them. In truth, there are probably many different pictures of the self which could, and do, stand behind this second truism. It is not possible to consider all of these alternatives here. Instead I will concentrate on one very common understanding of what is going on in such cases, trying to uncover the general picture of the self which stands behind it. I choose this particular reading of the truism not only because it is so common, but also because it is the reading most directly at

---

[7] Frankfurt, 'Identification and Wholeheartedness', p. 163.
[8] Frankfurt, 'Identification and Wholeheartedness', p. 170.

odds with the picture of the self developed by Frankfurt, and has served as a source of objections to his view.

When we say that a person is truly herself when she fails at self-control, we are very often thinking of a person who has a relatively coherent, persistent and longstanding set of desires which she rejects as improper or distasteful, and so actively suppresses. The dynamic here is a recurrent theme, among other places, in a wide range of popular entertainment. Musical comedy is a particularly rich source of such figures – Marian the librarian from *the Music Man*, and Sister Sarah from *Guys and Dolls*, both represent canonical versions of this character. In each case, a charming n'er-do-well breaks through the woman's defences in such a way that her more fun-loving, accepting, and romantic self finally finds expression. In these cases we are meant to view the breakthrough as a triumph. Inside each of these rigid women was a self, warm and full of life, just waiting to be released. A similar version of the same phenomenon can be found in many ordinary cases of conformity. Here we can think of someone who takes on the persona of the urban sophisticate – living where such people should live, eating what they should eat, seeing the films they should see and listening to the music they should listen to. We can imagine that none of this captures this man's natural tastes and desires, but only his idea of what those tastes and desires *should* be. We typically say that such a person is trying to be 'someone he is not'. If his friends from the old neighborhood should get a hold of him and induce him to indulge in a night of chips and beer and the music he enjoys without effort we view this as liberating for him – these are people with whom he can 'just be himself.'

What, then, is the picture of the self lying behind these familiar cases of self-suppression and liberation? The basic idea, it seems, is that the self is comprised of a set of natural inclinations and traits. When we express these in action we are being ourselves, and when we try to hide them in favor of others which are less natural, we are not. But more must be said about these 'natural' inclinations and traits – how we identify them, and in what sense they are natural. One approach might be to say that whatever desires or inclinations we experience spontaneously are part of the true self. This does not, however, seem to be the idea standing behind the cases we are considering. Those who hold this picture of the self could, for instance, agree with Frankfurt on cases of addiction and compulsion. There seems no inclination to applaud the breakthrough of the unwilling addict's suppressed desires when he breaks down and buys some crack. Nor do we need such dramatic cases to make the point. A one-time impulse to buy a sailboat that quickly fades and does not return may tell us *something* about a person, but probably does not represent anything deep about her true self.

A full account of what makes an inclination or trait 'natural' to a person in the relevant sense, and so part of herself, would require a great deal more analysis than can be provided here. It is, however, possible to outline some of the basic requirements that would undoubtedly be part of such a view. First, the inclinations that are going to constitute part of someone's true self must be relatively stable, coherent, and powerful. Second, they must not have their origin in an obvious physical or psychological pathology. Here I have in mind the cases on which this picture of the self and Frankfurt's agree – brain tumors, physical addictions, obsessive-compulsive disorder, and similar sources of impulsive desire.[9]

The final requirement is probably the most important, and also the hardest to define. The intuition behind it is that self-defining inclinations are not just desires for some very specific or concrete state of affairs, but also for a way of being or a type of life. They need not appear in this guise, however. They can take the form of specific desires, but are taken (either implicitly or explicitly) to represent something more. An example will help to clarify this requirement. Our sophisticated urbanite experiences and repudiates a craving for potato chips. His repudiation of this desire, however, is quite different from that of the person who simply decides for health reasons to eat a low fat or low sodium diet. The sophisticated urbanite wants not to be *the kind of person* who likes potato chips, while the healthy eater wants simply not to eat them. This distinction is already present in Frankfurt's position. Higher-order attitudes of endorsement and repudiation are generally going to be directed not only at first-order desires themselves, but

---

[9] Many would want to add that to be part of the self inclinations must also not result from pathological socialization. If the pathology here is extreme – brainwashing, torture and the like – this is fairly unproblematic. If, however, we try to include more subtle types of social pathology – such as ordinary forms of injustice and oppression, the case becomes very complex. To keep things simple I will stay with the less controversial version of the picture I am developing, which does not preclude the fact that we can have natural inclinations which are the result of socialization, even in less-than-perfect societies. There will be more on the intuitions I am setting aside here in later sections.

at the kind of person or life these desires represent. This requirement merely taps into this distinction by saying that the relevant
sorts of inclinations – the ones which are suppressed when a
person fails to be herself in this way – will be understood under
this description.

I will call inclinations which meet the above requirements
'robust' inclinations. The picture of the self which underlies our
second truism – at least one such picture – is that the self consists
in a person's robust inclinations. All such inclinations are part of
what can be called, in this context, a person's 'nature'. Since this
view holds that we fail to be ourselves when we fail to express some
part of our nature, I call it the 'self-expression' account of the
self, in contrast to Frankfurt's 'self-control' account. These two
accounts are, at least on the surface, in opposition to one another,
and indeed the basic sentiments behind the self-expression view
have served as a source of objections to Frankfurt's picture. One
early example of such an objection can be found in Marilyn
Friedman's discussion of a woman who has been taught that 'a
woman's place is in the home' and accepts that teaching. This
woman, however, experiences intense unhappiness and frustration trying to fulfil her role. In such a case, Friedman argues, the
woman's true desires are for a life outside of the home, despite
her higher-order repudiation of those desires.[10]

The basic idea behind Friedman's case can easily be turned into
an example which parallels the structure of Frankfurt's case of the
unwilling addict, and so highlights the tension between the two
views. Imagine a woman in a traditional American town in the
1950's who is wholeheartedly committed to fulfilling her duties as
a wife and mother as understood by the standards of her social
context. She is, however, frequently troubled by desires to take
courses at the local college, spend time with her friends, apply for
part-time jobs, or get involved in political causes. As powerful and
persistent as these desires are, this woman does her best to resist
them. She views them as selfish and unfeminine, and struggles
hard to keep them at bay. Just as the unwilling addict might use
methadone to resist his cravings, the 50's wife might use Valium.
And just as the addict might cut off contact with his old friends
to keep from falling back into his addiction, so might the 50's
wife cut off contact with 'progressive' friends who encourage her

---

[10]   Marilyn Friedman, 'Autonomy and the Split-Level Self', *Southern Journal of Philosophy*,
Spring 1986; 24, p. 31.

to explore her interests. Since the example of the 50's wife is devised to exactly parallel the case of the unwilling addict, Frankfurt will have to say that she is being herself in repudiating her desires for a life outside the home, and that those desires are not truly hers. If we accept the intuition that the 50's wife is failing to be herself in fulfilling her traditional role – and that she is herself when she breaks out of it – this case seems to present a counterexample to Frankfurt's account of the self. Considering how Frankfurt might respond to this example will help us to get clearer on the main features of these two pictures of the self.

III

In response to the case of the 50's wife presented as a counterexample to his account of the self, Frankfurt might well begin by reminding us just how strong a condition wholeheartedness is. The case stipulates that the 50's wife is wholeheartedly committed to her traditional role. To be sure we are clear on just what this means, it is important to know that Frankfurt allows that a person can be *mistaken* in the belief that she is wholehearted. In 'The Faintest Passion' he describes the difference between real and apparent satisfaction, and so between real and apparent wholeheartedness. He says that 'a person may make the judgment that he is well enough off; and on that basis he may decide to refrain from doing anything to improve his situation. Making this judgment or this decision does not, however, either make him satisfied or entail that he is satisfied'. This behavior, he says, merely simulates satisfaction, and 'to simulate satisfaction is not the same as being satisfied. A person is actually satisfied only when the equilibrium is not contrived or imposed but is integral to his psychic condition – that is, when that condition is settled and unreserved *apart from any effort by him to make it so*'.[11]

If we imagine the 50's wife as wholehearted, then, we must imagine that she effortlessly remains steadfast in the higher-order repudiation of the desires for a less traditional role. In particular, this means that when she struggles to resist these desires – or even when she succumbs to them – she never changes her mind about their undesirability. We must imagine this woman wholly uncon-

---

[11] Harry Frankfurt, 'The Faintest Passion', p. 104.

flicted about her wish not to give in to these temptations; she is
fighting the desires themselves and not the impulse to view them
as worthy. The wholehearted 50's wife does not sometimes wonder
whether it is really right for her to be shut off from the world in
this way, or think that perhaps her devotion to being a good wife
and mother should not guide her life in the way it does. She never
wavers on these points, and her steadfastness here is not the result
of effort or Valium (which only helps her to implement the
desires she wholeheartedly endorses). When we imagine this
woman giving in and signing up for a class, or joining a political
cause, we must imagine not just that she feels guilty about what
she is doing – for that is consistent with ambivalence – but that
she feels out of control, at the mercy of irresistible forces.

This reminder of what wholehearted identification entails
helps to make the claim that the 50's wife is indeed being herself
in fulfilling her traditional role more plausible, but it is not clear
that it entirely puts to rest the intuitions pulling in the other direction. A proponent of the self-expression view might protest that
even if she meets the strong conditions of wholeheartedness, we
have reason to believe that the 50's wife is not being herself
when she sticks to her traditional role. We can tell that she is not,
according to this view, because she is so miserable and depressed.
This woman, as described in the original case, suffers a type of
frustration and despair characteristic of suppressing robust
desires. It is thus an important feature of the self-expression view,
that failing to be oneself carries a significant cost. Consider
Friedman's analysis in her version of the case of the 50's wife. She
suggests that no matter how wholehearted this woman's commitment to her traditional role, the misery and frustration she experiences in trying to fulfil this role should make her rethink this
commitment. 'Her frustration, grief, and depression, and the
motivations to change her life which spring from these sources,
may be her only reliable guide,' says Friedman, to what she really
wants.[12]

The basic assumption, then, is that a particular kind of malaise
is symptomatic of suppressing one's robust inclinations. Of
course, there is always a certain amount of frustration which
results from unfulfilled desires, but in the sorts of cases we have
been discussing the unhappiness runs deeper. This is not to say

[12]   Marilyn Friedman, 'Autonomy and the Split-Level Self', p. 31.

that suppressing any part of one's nature will automatically lead to pervasive depression. The depths of one's despair will depend upon the depth and significance of the inclinations being suppressed, and how thoroughly unexpressed one's nature is. It is also not to say that there are no other causes of deep unhappiness, nor that there can never be good reasons for repression (more of this later). The idea, however, is that there is a peculiar kind of frustration, anxiety, and emptiness associated with suppressing one's true nature. This is an unhappiness which, e.g., Nietzsche and Freud portray as stemming not only from the failure to satisfy desires, but from a denial of one's own nature. When a person's failure to express her nature is severe enough, she is just 'going through the motions' of having a life, and that life will seem empty or meaningless. To be repressed is to be shut off and alienated from one's own life, and where we see psychological signs of such alienation, we have reason to suppose that a person is not being herself. Since these kinds of psychological symptoms seem completely compatible with wholeheartedness – as the case of the 50's wife demonstrates – Frankfurt's view fails to fully capture what it means to be oneself.

In response to this statement of the difficulty, a defender of the self-control view might insist that being oneself and being happy are not the same thing. It is important to understand that the claim that the 50's wife is being herself in fulfilling her traditional role does not require a proponent of this view to deny that there is something wrong with her situation. She is clearly not happy or fulfilled, and it is regrettable that this is her situation since in *some* sense she has the resources, if not the will, to make her plight better. What is wrong with her situation, however, is not that she fails to be herself, but rather that she has been made into someone who, in being herself, is unhappy and unfulfilled. This is particularly disturbing because we can so easily see an alternate way in which her identity might have developed which would have left her in much better shape. The self she has constituted is a frustrated, traditional wife and mother. Had she developed somewhat differently, she might perhaps have constituted herself as a more actualized and thriving person-in-the-world. The point about her despair is real and significant, a defender of the self-control view could argue, but not a fact about who she *is*.

The dialectic between these two views could, of course, continue, and there is no obvious way to resolve this disagreement. Both accounts seem to capture a legitimate sense of what it means for a person to be herself. Surely Frankfurt is right that in one sense being oneself requires that a person have command of her own will. Should the 50's wife act out against her traditional role despite having resolved not to do so, there is a clear sense in which she is not doing what she most wants to do – a sense in which she *is* like the unwilling addict. No one would view this as a particularly healthy or actualizing way to live a life. At the same time, it also seems right that being oneself involves expressing one's nature. There is a clear sense in which the 50's wife, when she *is* in command of her will, is using it keep her from being herself. All of which is to say that she is being herself in one way, but not in another. Having realized this, one option is just to stop the dialectic, accepting the fact that we use the term 'self' in more than one way – hardly a surprising result. Our discussion reveals, however, that there is an important point of contact between these two views of the self and this points to a more integrated view with broader application.

IV

While the self-control and self-expression views capture different senses of what it is to be oneself – senses which typically apply in different domains – they do have an important point of contact. In both cases there is an underlying presupposition that being oneself is an essential part of living a meaningful or fulfilling life. The main difference between these views is that they focus on different ways in which the capacity for such a life might be threatened. The self-control account develops from the insight that an uncontrolled life lacks meaning, while the self-expression account grows from the same recognition about a repressed life. The connection between the self-expression account and a meaningful life is evident from the discussion of the objection this view of the self raises against Frankfurt. This objection was based on the fact that the emptiness and alienation experienced by the 50's wife showed that she was not being herself, and this emptiness was linked to a failure of self-expression. The role of meaning in the self-control view is less evident, and it is worth discussing in some detail.

Frankfurt's view again serves as an exemplary representative of this general picture. Issues of flourishing and living a meaningful life enter into Frankfurt's account at several levels. An important feature of his argument for his conception of autonomy is his emphasis on the damaging consequences of ambivalence. When a person is unable to take sides between conflicting desires, she is pulled in different directions, paralyzed, and can take no effective action. He tells us that

> the opportunity to act in accordance with his own inclinations is a doubtful asset for an individual whose will is so divided that he is moved both to decide for a certain alternative and to decide against it. Neither of the alternatives can satisfy him, since each entails the frustration of the other. The fact that he is free to choose between them is likely only to make his anguish more poignant and more intense.[13]

Ambivalence, says Frankfurt, is a 'disease of the will' which no one could want for its own sake.[14] And when we do achieve wholeheartedness, acting against our wholehearted commitment is a self-destructive act – an infliction of 'drastic psychic injuries'.[15] If we cannot unify our wills, our lives will be at best empty, and at worst an utter disaster.

The role of flourishing and meaning in Frankfurt's conception of the self becomes even clearer in his later work on caring and love.[16] In this work Frankfurt discusses the way in which our wills are constrained when we care about something or love it. The 'care' and 'love' he describes here are not so much emotions or passions, but rather denote the way in which our wills are constrained by certain particular attachments. When we love something (a person, cause, profession, or country), we are committed to its flourishing, and find we cannot will ourselves to act otherwise. In this way, what we care about constrains us. Love and care

---

[13]   Harry Frankfurt, 'The Faintest Passion', p. 104.

[14]   David Velleman has offered an interesting objection to Frankfurt's idea of wholeheartedness based on the claim that the drive to wholeheartedness in can cause more damage than ambivalence. Frankfurt's response to this charge rests on the distinction between acknowledging that a motivation is part of one's psychological history and thinking of it as internal to the self. This interchange is too complicated to discuss here, but it at least shows that the issue of flourishing and meaning do indeed play a role in Frankfurt's view. For more details see Velleman's 'Identification and Identity' and Frankfurt's reply in Sarah Buss and Lee Overton, eds. *Contours of Agency* (Cambridge: The MIT Press, 2002), pp. 91–128.

[15]   Harry Frankfurt, 'Autonomy, Necessity and Love' in *Necessity, Volition, and Love*, p. 139.

[16]   In some of his work he talks about 'what we care about', in others about the volitional necessities defined by 'what we love'. While there is much that might be said about the connection between these two ideas, for present purposes they are sufficiently similar that I will treat them as synonomous.

are, however, quite different from other sorts of necessitation in that we identify with and endorse the constraints they impose. In this way the constraints of love are more like autonomous choices than compulsions.

What is most important for present purposes is Frankfurt's repeated emphasis on the importance that caring and loving themselves have for us. Far from it being a burden to have our wills constrained in this way, it is central to what makes life worth living. Frankfurt argues that we do not care about things because they are independently important to us, or worthy of care. Rather, they are important *because* we care about them. It is through our coming to love and care about things that important and meaningful activity enters our lives. When we care about something, our action is directed in purposeful ways. The value of such activity is something he emphasizes in 'On the Usefulness of Final Ends.' There he points to the intrinsic value of means to our ends as a source of purposeful work. He tells us that '*people* aim also at having useful work. Moreover, they do not desire useful work only because they desire its products. In fact, useful work is among their final ends. They desire it for its own sake, since without it life is empty and vain.'[17] Because of this, he says, we should choose final ends which are valuable to us not only for their own sake, but which are met by means that are complex and enjoyable.

The very notion and possibility of useful work comes from our capacity to love, and in 'On Caring' he tells us that 'without loving in one or more of its several modes life for us would be intolerably unshaped and empty. For our own sakes, we *need* to love; otherwise, our lives will be miserably deprived.'[18] Frankfurt thus makes it clear how important it is for us to have meaningful lives. More to the point, since this meaning is connected to loving, and loving has to do with the structure of the will, this meaning is inherently tied to our identities. He tells us that 'the authority for the lover of the claims that are made upon him by his love is the authority of his own essential nature as a person. It is, in other words, the authority over him of the essential nature of his own individual will.'[19]

---

[17] Harry Frankfurt, 'On the Usefulness of Final Ends', in *Necessity, Volition and Love*, p. 91.

[18] Harry Frankfurt, 'On Caring', in *Necessity, Volition and Love*, p. 174

[19] Harry Frankfurt, 'Autonomy, Necessity and Love', p. 138.

This notion of flourishing, in the sense of living a meaningful or purposeful life, thus seems to offer a connection between the two conceptions of the self we have been considering. This is not to say that somehow the 'right' account of the self must define it in terms of such flourishing. It is quite a strong requirement, and we must leave open a real sense in which people can be selves even when they feel empty or unfulfilled. To see that there is a legitimate notion of the self at work here, however, recall our starting point. The original idea was that being a self is something which is, so far as we know, a peculiar prerogative of human beings. We thus looked to the unique features of human lives to define the self. Frankfurt focused on the possibility of autonomous action as this defining feature. What we have seen, however, is that it is also a central (and related) feature of human life that we seek not only to *direct* our lives, but to direct them in a way that constitutes purposeful and meaningful activity. The picture of humans as meaning-seekers is tapped into by both of the accounts of the self we have been considering, and in this way connects them. In the final section I will consider how these two views might be integrated into a broader view.

V

The previous section showed that the self-control and self-expression pictures of what it is to be oneself can be seen as addressing different ways in which we can become alienated from our lives, and so fail to be ourselves. The self-control view expresses the fact that we are alienated from our actions when we cannot control or direct them; the self-expression view that we are alienated when our lives do not express our natures. To integrate these two views we should thus attempt to develop an account of being oneself that avoids both threats. One natural idea of how to achieve this integration is simply to add together the requirements of the two views we have been discussing. This would yield an account of being oneself which sees the self as constituted by wholehearted identification with our robust, natural inclinations. Identification is required to make us active with respect to our lives and distinguish us from animals who act on instinct. Constraints on legitimate candidates for self-building would solve the problem we found in cases like that of the 50's wife. It may seem, moreover, that the basic components for developing this sort of view are already present in Frankfurt's account. As we have seen, he emphasizes that it is not possible for us to care about or whole-heartedly commit to any motivation we choose. The capacity for wholeheartedness will be determined by contingent facts about one's history. It would be very convenient if the limitations on wholeheartedness were set by our robust inclinations. Cases like the 50's wife show that this is not automatically the case, but it is tempting to think that we could tweak the notion of wholeheart-edness to make it so, and in this way integrate the insights of the two views.

This straightforward integration, however, fails to take either view seriously enough in its own terms. For this view to work, the contribution of the self-control view would need to be limited to putting a stamp of approval and ownership on our robust incli-nations, and the contribution of the self-expression view to pro-viding a list of legitimate candidates for this stamp. But each view demands something stronger. Frankfurt's analysis – especially in its relation to flourishing and meaning – suggests that we *cannot* express all of our robust inclinations. The romantic picture of a well-formed self just waiting to be set free is a nice one, but unlikely to be true. Our natures will more plausibly involve con-tradictory inclinations, and self-destructive ones. Unless we repress at least some of our natures we are likely, as Frankfurt says, to act in ways that are incoherent or self-undermining. Fully expressing our natures really might threaten to negate the possi-bility of living a meaningful life. Sometimes we need to bend to our own yoke. If not from experience, then at least from Freud, we know that the need for some level of repression is a fact of life.

The self-expression view also requires more than this simple attempt at integration would provide. The challenge it poses to Frankfurt, and the self-control picture more generally, runs deeper than that. The self-control view insists that we must be active with respect to any inclination which can rightly be con-sidered our own. To the extent that we are passive with respect to our actions, according to this view, they merely occur in us and are not yet ours. The ideals of this view are thus activity and unity. The self-expression picture, however, suggests the need for a certain amount of passivity, and a certain toleration of ambiva-lence. In order to be ourselves on this view, we must express our natures. It is well-known, however, that our natures are not always transparent to us. We do not always know what will constitute meaningful and purposeful activity for us, and introspection alone will not always be enough to make this clear. Living a human life thus involves a certain amount of experimentation – trying out different possibilities, following out inchoate inclinations, and trusting ourselves sometimes to overthrow a standing commitment to see if something else might work better. Nor should these routes to self-discovery always be considered something we *do* in Frankfurt's sense. Sometimes we need to just 'let go', sitting back and allowing ourselves to be receptive to what we learn about ourselves when we relinquish control. While resolution is usually ultimately desirable, an overhasty cutting off of options and a conservative nature can keep a person from discovering the life that suits him best. Frankfurt does allow that there might be reasons sometimes to be ambivalent. What we see here, however, is not just a case for sadly resigning ourselves to a necessary evil. Instead, these observations suggest that the will plays a quite different part in allowing one to be oneself than the self-control view says it does.

Frequently analogies are made between selves and states, and this sort of analogy may clarify issues here. The self-control account as developed by Frankfurt can be seen as a Hobbesian picture of self-government. The danger of disintegration is taken to be so pressing that the main objective is to resolve conflicts decisively. The only legitimate authority, moreover, is the authority of the sovereign, and so, as Frankfurt often says, no desires have authority for us except those upon which authority is conferred by wholehearted identification. The self-expression view accuses this picture of over-estimating the danger of internal civil war. In extreme cases like addiction, the need for firm commitments may indeed be real. But in times of relative inner peace, it is worth buying a bit of liberty at the cost of a threat of small instabilities. Frankfurt might be right that freedom has little value if we do not know what we want, but it is also true that stability is of little value if it means subordinating oneself to a repressive sovereign. The self-expression view thus gives a presumptive authority to our robust inclinations. In its extreme form, however, this alternative view threatens anarchy. Giving equal authority to all of these inclinations and setting no constraints might well lead to the sort of disintegration the self-control view reacts against. If we are to discover our natures through experimentation, then, we had better set limits on that experimentation. The role of the will will thus be less to place a stamp on approved passions, as it would be in the simple integration of these two views, and more to set up guidelines within which we can safely be more passive.

The approach that will stave off both threats will thus be more like a liberal democracy than a Hobbesian sovereign. Insofar as is compatible with still living a meaningful life, we should try to give free rein to our robust inclinations. The optimal degree of liberty will depend upon the nature of the inclinations (experimenting with drug use or infidelity is often more dangerous to living an optimal life than experimenting with graduate school or writing a novel), and on one's environment (the real options available to the 50's wife might be such that the most meaningful life possible for her will consist in her traditional role). The task of being oneself thus involves seeking the appropriate balance between constraint and liberty – between self-expression and self-control. As in Frankfurt's view, constituting oneself as a self involves making distinctions and choices which limit self-expression. However, this integrated approach differs from Frankfurt's in two important respects. First, our robust inclinations are to be given presumptive authority even when we do not identify with them, and so the threshold for excluding them will be higher. The will gets its authority in part from its capacity to represent our inclinations in an orderly fashion rather than being the sole source of authority. Second, the work of shaping a life is less of a task of micro-management. It is less about directly settling conflicts than about establishing safe boundaries within which these conflicts can be allowed to play themselves out.

The self-control and self-expression views each capture important insights about what it is to be oneself, and to be *a* self. There is a need for each of these views, and a domain in which each gives the 'right' answer about who one is. If, however, we define being a self in terms of living the kind of life characteristic of, and seemingly peculiar to, humans, the view that captures the full range of intuitions will be more complicated than either. What is peculiar to us is that we *can* be alienated from our lives, and we seek not to be. To be ourselves we must govern our lives in a way that avoids this alienation – carefully balancing the demands of self-expression and self-control.[20]

---

[20] In thinking about these issues I have been aided by many friends and colleagues. I would like especially to thank Tony Laden, John Santiago, and Marc Slors.

CHAPTER 4

AGAINST NARRATIVITY

Galen Strawson

1 Talk of narrative is intensely fashionable in a wide variety of disciplines including philosophy, psychology, theology, anthropology, sociology, political theory, literary studies, religious studies, psychotherapy and even medicine. There is widespread agreement that human beings typically see or live or experience their lives as a narrative or story of some sort, or at least as a collection of stories. I'll call this the *psychological Narrativity thesis,* using the word 'Narrative' with a capital letter to denote a specifically psychological property or outlook. The psychological Narrativity thesis is a straightforwardly empirical, descriptive thesis about the way ordinary human beings actually experience their lives. This is how we are, it says, this is our nature.

The psychological Narrativity thesis is often coupled with a normative thesis, which I'll call the *ethical Narrativity thesis.* This states that experiencing or conceiving one's life as a narrative is a good thing; a richly Narrative outlook is essential to a well-lived life, to true or full personhood.

The descriptive thesis and the normative thesis have four main combinations. One may, to begin, think the descriptive thesis true and the normative one false. One may think that we are indeed deeply Narrative in our thinking and that it's not a good thing. The protagonist of Sartre's novel *La nausée* holds something like this view.[1] So do the Stoics, as far as I can see.

Second, and contrariwise, one may think the descriptive thesis false and the normative one true. One may grant that we are not all naturally Narrative in our thinking but insist that we should be, and need to be, in order to live a good life. There are versions of this view in Plutarch[2] and a host of present-day writings.

Third, one may think both theses are true: one may think that all normal non-pathological human beings are naturally Narra-

---

[1] Sartre 1938.
[2] See e.g. 100AD, pp. 214–7 (473B–474B).

tive and also that Narrativity is crucial to a good life. This is the dominant view in the academy today, followed by the second view. It does not entail that everything is as it should be; it leaves plenty of room for the idea that many of us would profit from being more Narrative than we are, and the idea that we can get our self-narratives wrong in one way or another.

Finally, one may think that both theses are false. This is my view. I think the current widespread acceptance of the third view is regrettable. It's just not true that there is only one good way for human beings to experience their being in time. There are deeply non-Narrative people and there are good ways to live that are deeply non-Narrative. I think the second and third views hinder human self-understanding, close down important avenues of thought, impoverish our grasp of ethical possibilities, needlessly and wrongly distress those who do not fit their model, and are potentially destructive in psychotherapeutic contexts.

2 The first thing I want to put in place is a distinction between one's experience of oneself when one is considering oneself principally as a human being taken as a whole, and one's experience of oneself when one is considering oneself principally as an inner mental entity or 'self' of some sort – I'll call this one's self-experience. When Henry James says, of one of his early books, 'I think of . . . the masterpiece in question . . . as the work of quite another person than myself . . . a rich . . . relation, say, who . . . suffers me still to claim a shy fourth cousinship',[3] he has no doubt that he is the same human being as the author of that book, but he does not feel he is the same self or person as the author of that book. It is this phenomenon of experiencing oneself as a self that concerns me here. One of the most important ways in which people tend to think of themselves (quite independently of religious belief) is as things whose persistence conditions are not obviously or automatically the same as the persistence conditions of a human being considered as a whole. Petrarch, Proust, Parfit and thousands of others have given this idea vivid expression. I'm going to take its viability for granted and set up another distinction – between 'Episodic' and 'Diachronic' self-experience – in terms of it.

---

[3]   1915: 562–3.

3 The basic form of Diachronic self-experience is that

[**D**] one naturally figures oneself, considered as a self, as something that was there in the (further) past and will be there in the (further) future

– something that has relatively long-term diachronic continuity, something that persists over a long stretch of time, perhaps for life. I take it that many people are naturally Diachronic, and that many who are Diachronic are also Narrative in their outlook on life.

If one is Episodic, by contrast,

[**E**] one does not figure oneself, considered as a self, as something that was there in the (further) past and will be there in the (further) future.

One has little or no sense that the self that one is was there in the (further) past and will be there in the future, although one is perfectly well aware that one has long-term continuity considered as a whole human being. Episodics are likely to have no particular tendency to see their life in Narrative terms.[4]

The Episodic and Diachronic styles of temporal being are radically opposed, but they are not absolute or exceptionless. Predominantly Episodic individuals may sometimes connect to charged events in their pasts in such a way that they feel that those events happened to them – embarrassing memories are a good example – and anticipate events in their futures in such a way that they think that those events are going to happen to them – thoughts of future death can be a good example. So too predominantly Diachronic individuals may sometimes experience an Episodic lack of linkage with well remembered parts of their past. It may be that the basic Episodic disposition is less common in human beings than the basic Diachronic disposition, but many factors may induce variations in individuals. I take it that the fundamentals of temporal temperament are genetically determined, and that we have here to do with a deep 'individual difference variable', to put it in the language of experimental psychology. Individual variation in time-style, Episodic or Diachronic, Narrative or non-Narrative, will be found across all cultures, so that the same general spread will be found in a so-called 'revenge culture',

---

[4] The Episodic/Diachronic distinction is not the same thing as the Narrative/non-Narrative distinction, as will emerge; but there are marked correlations between them.

with its essentially Diachronic emphasis, as in a more happy-go-lucky culture.[5] Compatibly with that, one's exact position in Episodic/Diachronic/Narrative/non-Narrative state-space may vary significantly over time according to what one is doing or thinking about, one's state of health, and so on; and it may change markedly with increasing age.

Diachronics and Episodics are likely to misunderstand one another badly. Diachronics may feel that there is something chilling, empty and deficient about the Episodic life. They may fear it, although it is no less full or emotionally articulated than the Diachronic life, no less thoughtful or sensitive, no less open to friendship, love and loyalty. And certainly the two forms of life differ significantly in their ethical and emotional form. But it would be a great mistake to think that the Episodic life is bound to be less vital or in some way less engaged, or less humane, or less humanly fulfilled. If Heideggerians think that Episodics are necessarily 'inauthentic' in their experience of being in time, so much the worse for their notion of authenticity.[6] And if Episodics are moved to respond by casting aspersions on the Diachronic life – finding it somehow macerated or clogged, say, or excessively self-concerned, inauthentically second-order – they too will be mistaken if they think it an essentially inferior form of human life.

There is one sense in which Episodics are by definition more located in the present than Diachronics, so far as their self-experience is concerned, but it does not follow, and is not true, that Diachronics are less present in the present moment than Episodics, any more than it follows, or is true, that in the Episodic life the present is somehow less informed by or responsible to the past than it is in the Diachronic life. What is true is that the informing and the responsiveness have different characteristics and different experiential consequences in the two cases. Faced with sceptical Diachronics, who insist that Episodics are (essentially) dysfunctional in the way they relate to their own past, Episodics will reply that the past can be present or alive in the present without being present or alive *as* the past. The past can be alive – arguably more genuinely alive – in the present simply in so far as it has helped to shape the way one is in the present,

[5] Although a culture could in theory exert significant selective pressure on a psychological trait. For descriptions of revenge culture see Blumenfeld 2003.
[6] Cf. e.g. Heidegger 1927.

just as musicians' playing can incorporate and body forth their past practice without being mediated by any explicit memory of it. What goes for musical development goes equally for ethical development, and Rilke's remarks on poetry and memory, which have a natural application to the ethical case, suggest one way in which the Episodic attitude to the past may have an advantage over the Diachronic: 'For the sake of a single poem', he writes, 'you must have . . . many . . . memories. . . . And yet it is not enough to have memories. . . . For the memories themselves are not important.' They give rise to a good poem 'only when they have changed into our very blood, into glance and gesture, and are nameless, no longer to be distinguished from ourselves.'[7]

4 How do Episodicity and Diachronicity relate to Narrativity? Suppose that being Diachronic is at least necessary for being Narrative. Since it's true by definition that if you're Diachronic you're not Episodic and conversely, it follows that if you're Episodic you're not Narrative. But I think that the strongly Episodic life is one normal, non-pathological form of life for human beings, and indeed one good form of life for human beings, one way to flourish. So I reject both the psychological Narrativity thesis and the normative, ethical Narrativity thesis.

I need to say more about the Episodic life, and since I find myself to be relatively Episodic, I'll use myself as an example. I have a past, like any human being, and I know perfectly well that I have a past. I have a respectable amount of factual knowledge about it, and I also remember some of my past experiences 'from the inside', as philosophers say. And yet I have absolutely no sense of my life as a narrative with form, or indeed as a narrative without form. Absolutely none. Nor do I have any great or special interest in my past. Nor do I have a great deal of concern for my future.

That's one way to put it – to speak in terms of limited interest. Another way is to say that it seems clear to me, when I am expe-

---

[7] Among those whose writings show them to be markedly Episodic I propose Michel de Montaigne, the Earl of Shaftesbury, Stendhal, Hazlitt, Ford Madox Ford, Virginia Woolf, Borges, Fernando Pessoa, Iris Murdoch (a strongly Episodic person who is a natural story teller), Freddie Ayer, Goronwy Rees, Bob Dylan. Proust is another candidate, in spite of his memoriousness (which may be inspired by his Episodicity); also Emily Dickinson. On the other side – to begin with – Plato, St. Augustine, Heidegger, Tom Nagel, probably Nietzsche, all the champions of of narrative and Narrativity in the current ethico-psychological debate, and some of my closest friends.

riencing or apprehending myself as a self, that the remoter past or future in question is not my past or future, although it is certainly the past or future of GS the human being. This is more dramatic, but I think it is equally correct, when I am figuring myself as a self. I have no significant sense that *I* – the I now considering this question – was there in the further past. And it seems clear to me that this is not a failure of feeling. It is, rather, a registration of a fact about what I am – about what the thing that is currently considering this problem is.

I will use 'I*' to represent: that which I now experience myself to be when I'm apprehending myself specifically as an inner mental presence or self. 'I*' comes with a large family of cognate forms – 'me*', 'my*', 'you*' 'oneself*', 'themselves*', and so on. The metaphysical presumption built into these terms is that they succeed in making genuine reference to an inner mental something that is reasonably called a 'self'. But it doesn't matter whether or not the presumption is correct.[8]

So: it's clear to me that events in my remoter past didn't happen to me*. But what does this amount to? It certainly doesn't mean that I don't have any autobiographical memories of these past experiences. I do. Nor does it mean that my autobiographical memories don't have what philosophers call a 'from-the-inside' character. Some of them do. And they are certainly the experiences of the human being that I am. It does not, however, follow from this that I experience them as having happened to me*, or indeed that they did happen to me*. They certainly do not present as things that happened to me*, and I think I'm strictly, literally correct in thinking that they did not happen to me*.

– That can't be right. If one of my remembered experiences has a from-the-inside character it must – by definition – be experienced as something that happened to me.*

This may seem plausible at first, but it's a mistake: the from-the-inside character of a memory can detach completely from any sense that one is the subject of the remembered experience. My memory of falling out of a boat has an essentially from-the-inside character, visually (the water rushing up to meet me), kinaes-

---

[8]   The term 'I*' and its cognates can function in phenomenological contexts to convey the content of a form of experience that incorporates the presumption whether or not the presumption is actually correct. I'll omit the '*' when it's not necessary.

thetically, proprioceptively, and so on.[9] It certainly does not follow that it carries any feeling or belief that what is remembered happened to me*, to that which I now apprehend myself to be when I am apprehending myself specifically as a self.

This doesn't follow even when emotion figures in the from-the-inside character of the autobiographical memory. The inference from [1] The memory has a from-the-inside character in emotional respects to [2] The memory is experienced as something that happened to me* is simply not valid, although for many people [1] and [2] are often or usually true together.

For me this is a plain fact of experience. I'm well aware that my past is mine in so far as I am a human being, and I fully accept that there's a sense in which it has special relevance to me* now, including special emotional and moral relevance. At the same time I have no sense that I* was there in the past, and think it obvious that I* was not there, as a matter of metaphysical fact. As for my practical concern for my future, which I believe to be within the normal human range (low end), it is biologically – viscerally – grounded and autonomous in such a way that I can experience it as something immediately felt even though I have no significant sense that I* will be there in the future.

5 So much, briefly, for the Episodic life. What about the Narrative life? And what might it mean to say that human life is 'narrative' in nature? And must you be Diachronic to be Narrative? There are many questions.

One clear statement of the psychological Narrativity thesis is given by Roquentin in Sartre's novel *La nausée*:

> a man is always a teller of stories, he lives surrounded by his own stories and those of other people, he sees everything that happens to him *in terms of* these stories and he tries to live his life as if he were recounting it.[10]

Sartre sees the narrative, story-telling impulse as a defect, regrettable. He accepts the psychological Narrativity thesis while rejecting the ethical Narrativity thesis. He thinks human Narrativity is essentially a matter of bad faith, of radical (and typically irreme-

---

[9] It does not have any sort of 'from-the-outside' character (that would be a bit like my seeing a film of myself falling taken by a third party).

[10] 1938, p. 64. Sartre is as much concerned with relatively short-term passages of life as with life as a whole.

diable) inauthenticity, rather than as something essential for authenticity.

The pro-Narrative majority may concede to Sartre that Narrativity can go wrong while insisting that it's not all bad and that it is necessary for a good life. I'm with Sartre on the ethical issue, but I want now to consider some statements of the psychological Narrativity thesis. Oliver Sacks puts it by saying that 'each of us constructs and lives a "narrative" . . . this narrative *is* us, our identities'. The distinguished psychologist Jerry Bruner writes of 'the stories we tell about our lives', claiming that 'self is a perpetually rewritten story', and that 'in the end, we *become* the autobiographical narratives by which we "tell about" our lives'.[11] Dan Dennett claims that

> we are all virtuoso novelists, who find ourselves engaged in all sorts of behaviour, and we always try to put the best 'faces' on it we can. We try to make all of our material cohere into a single good story. And that story is our autobiography. The chief fictional character at the centre of that autobiography is one's self.[12]

Marya Schechtman goes further, twisting the ethical and the psychological Narrativity theses tightly together in a valuably forthright manner. A person, she says, 'creates his identity [only] by forming an autobiographical narrative – a story of his life'. One must be in possession of a full and 'explicit narrative [of one's life] to develop fully as a person'.[13]

Charles Taylor presents it this way: a 'basic condition of making sense of ourselves', he says, 'is that we grasp our lives in a *narrative*' and have an understanding of our lives 'as an unfolding story'. This is not, he thinks, 'an optional extra'; our lives exist 'in a space of questions, which only a coherent narrative can answer'.[14] He is backed up by Claire in Doug Copeland's novel *Generation X*: 'Claire . . . breaks the silence by saying that it's not healthy to live life as a succession of isolated little cool moments. "Either our lives become stories, or there's no way to get through them"'; but Taylor builds a lot more ethical weight into what's involved in getting through life. It is

[11] Sacks 1985, p. 110; Bruner 1987, pp. 11, 15, 12; 1994, p. 53.
[12] Dennett 1988, p. 1029.
[13] Schechtman 1997, pp. 93, 119.
[14] 1989, pp. 47, 52.

because we cannot but orient ourselves to the good, and hence determine our place relative to it and hence determine the direction of our lives, [that] we must inescapably understand our lives in narrative form, as a 'quest' [and] must see our lives in story.[15]

This, he says, is an 'inescapable structural requirement of human agency',[16] and Paul Ricoeur appears to concur:

How, indeed, could a subject of action give an ethical charac-ter to his or her own life taken as a whole if this life were not gathered together in some way, and how could this occur if not, precisely, in the form of a narrative?[17]

Here my main puzzlement is about what it might be to 'give an ethical character to [one's] own life taken as a whole' in some explicit way, and about why on earth, in the midst of the beauty of being, it should be thought to be important to do this. I think that those who think in this way are motivated by a sense of their own importance or significance that is absent in other human beings. Many of them, connectedly, have religious commitments. They are wrapped up in forms of religious belief that are – like almost all religious belief – really all about self.[18]

Alasdair MacIntyre is perhaps the founding figure in the modern Narrativity camp, and his view is similar to Taylor's. 'The unity of an individual life', he says, 'is the unity of a narrative embodied in a single life. To ask "What is the good for me?" is to ask how best I might live out that unity and bring it to comple-tion. . . .' The unity of a human life, he continues,

is the unity of a narrative quest . . . [and] the only criteria for success or failure in a human life as a whole are the criteria for success or failure in a narrated or to-be-narrated quest. . . . A quest for what? . . . a quest for the good . . . the good life for man is the life spent in seeking for the good life for man.[19]

---

[15] 1989, pp. 51–2. I reject the 'because' and the second 'hence'.
[16] 1989, p. 52.
[17] 1990, p. 158.
[18] Excessive self-concern is much more likely to be the cause of religious belief in someone who has come to religion than in someone who has been born into it. That does not change the fact that religious belief in general, ostensibly self-denying, is one of the fundamental vehicles of human narcissism.
[19] 1981, pp. 203–4.

MacIntyre's claim seems at first non-psychological: a good life is one that has narrative unity. But a good life is one spent seeking the good life, and there is a strong suggestion that seeking the good life requires taking up a Narrative perspective; in which case narrative unity requires Narrativity.

Is any of this true? I don't think so. It seems to me that Mac-Intyre, Taylor and all other supporters of the ethical Narrativity thesis are really just talking about themselves. It may be that what they are saying is true for them, both psychologically and ethically. This may be the best ethical project that people like themselves can hope to engage in.[20] But even if it is true for them it is not true for other types of ethical personality, and many are likely to be thrown right off their own truth by being led to believe that Narrativity is necessary for a good life. My own conviction is that the best lives almost never involve this kind of self-telling, and that we have here yet another deep divider of the human race.

When a Narrative like John Campbell claims that 'identity [through time] is central to what we care about in our lives: one thing I care about is what I have made of my life'[21], I'm as bewildered as Goronwy Rees when he writes

> For as long as I can remember it has always surprised and slightly bewildered me that other people should take it so much for granted that they each possess what is usually called 'a character'; that is to say, a personality [or personality-possessing self] with its own continuous history. . . . I have never been able to find anything of that sort in myself. . . . How much I admire those writers who are actually able to record the growth of what they call their personality, describe the conditions which determined its birth, lovingly trace the curve of its development. . . . For myself it would be quite impossible to tell such a story, because at no time in my life have I had that enviable sensation of constituting a continuous personality. . . . As a child this did not worry me, and if indeed I had known at that time of *Der Mann ohne Eigenschaften* [*The Man without Qualities*, a novel by Robert Musil], the man without qualities, I would have greeted him as my blood brother and rejoiced because I was

---

[20] One problem with it, and it is a deep problem, is that one is almost certain to get one's 'story' wrong, in some more or less sentimental way – unless, perhaps, one has the help of a truly gifted therapist.

[21] 1994, p. 190.

not alone in the world; as it was, I was content with a private fantasy of my own in which I figured as Mr. Nobody.[22]

Unlike Rees, I have a perfectly good grasp of myself as having a certain personality, but I'm completely uninterested in the answer to the question 'What has GS made of his life?', or 'What have I made of my life?'. I'm living it, and this sort of thinking about it is no part of it. This does not mean that I am in any way irresponsible. It is just that what I care about, in so far as I care about myself and my life, is how I am now. The way I am now is profoundly shaped by my past, but it is only the present shaping consequences of the past that matter, not the past as such. I agree with the Earl of Shaftesbury:

> The metaphysicians . . . affirm that if memory be taken away, the self is lost. [But] what matter for memory? What have I to do with that part? If, *whilst I am*, I am as I should be, what do I care more? And thus let me lose *self* every hour, and be twenty successive selfs, or new selfs, 'tis all one to me: so [long as] I lose not my opinion [i.e. my overall outlook, my character, my moral identity]. If I carry that with me 'tis I; all is well. . . . – The *now*, the *now*. Mind this: in this is all.[23]

I think, then, that the ethical Narrativity thesis is false, and that the psychological Narrativity thesis is also false in any non-trivial version. What do I mean by non-trivial? Well, if someone says, as some do, that making coffee is a narrative that involves Narrativity, because you have to think ahead, do things in the right order, and so on, and that everyday life involves many such narratives, then I take it the claim is trivial.[24]

Is there some burden on me to explain the popularity of the two theses, given that I think that they're false? Hardly. Theorizing human beings tend to favour false views in matters of this kind. I do, though, think that intellectual fashion is part of the explanation. I also suspect that those who are drawn to write on the subject of 'narrativity' tend to have strongly Diachronic and Narrative outlooks or personalities, and generalize from their own

---

[22] 1960, pp. 9–10.

[23] Shaftesbury 1698–1712, pp. 136–137; Epictetus is an important influence.

[24] Taylor is explicit that it is when I am not 'dealing with such trivial questions as where I shall go in the next five minutes but with the issue of my place relative to the good', that 'making sense of my present action . . . requires a narrative understanding of my life' (1989, p. 48).

case with that special, fabulously misplaced confidence that people feel when, considering elements of their own experience that are existentially fundamental for them, they take it that they must also be fundamental for everyone else.[25]

6 – *All very interesting, but what exactly is (upper-case) Narrativity? You still haven't addressed the question directly, and you're running out of time.*

Perhaps the first thing to say is that being Diachronic doesn't already entail being Narrative. There must be something more to experiencing one's life as a narrative than simply being Diachronic. For one can be Diachronic, naturally experiencing oneself(*) as something existing in the past and future without any particular sense of one's life as constituting a narrative.

– Fine, but you haven't told me what a (lower-case) narrative is either.

Well, the paradigm of a narrative is a conventional story told in words. I take the term to attribute – at the very least – a certain sort of *developmental* and hence temporal *unity* or *coherence* to the things to which it is standardly applied – lives, parts of lives, pieces of writing. So it doesn't apply to random or radically unconnected sequences of events even when they are sequentially and indeed contiguously temporally ordered, or to purely picaresque or randomly 'cut-up' pieces of writing.[26]

– This doesn't take us very far, because we still need to know what makes developmental unity or coherence in a life specifically narrative in nature. After all, there's a clear sense in which every human life is a developmental unity – a historical-characteral developmental unity as well as a biological one – just in being the life of a single human being. Putting aside cases of extreme insanity, any human life, even a highly disordered one, can be the subject of an outstanding biography that possesses all the narrative-unity-related virtues of that literary form. But if this sort of developmental unity is sufficient for narrative structure in the sense of the narrativity thesis, then the thesis is trivially true of all human beings. Actually, even dogs and horses can be the subject of excellent biographies.

---

[25] I think this may be the greatest single source of unhappiness in human intercourse.
[26] There are, however, many interesting complications. See *Life in Time*.

True. And this, I think, is why the distinctive claim of the defenders of the psychological Narrativity thesis is that for a life to be a narrative in the required sense it must be lived Narratively. The person whose life it is must see or feel it as a narrative, construe it as a narrative, live it as a narrative. One could put this roughly by saying that lower-case or 'objective' narrativity requires upper-case or 'subjective' Narrativity.[27]

– Now you're using the notion of upper-case psychological Narrativity to characterize the notion of lower-case 'objective' narrativity, and I still don't have a clear sense of what upper-case Narrativity is.

Well, it's not easy, but perhaps one can start from the idea of a *construction* in the sense of a construal. The Narrative outlook clearly involves putting some sort of construction – a unifying or form-finding construction – on the events of one's life, or parts of one's life. I don't think this construction need involve any clearly intentional activity, nor any departure from or addition to the facts. But the Narrative attitude must (as we have already agreed) amount to something more than a disposition to grasp one's life as a unity simply in so far as it is the life of a biologically single human being. Nor can it consist just in the ability to give a sequential record of the actual course of one's life –, the actual history of one's life – even if one's life does in fact exemplify a classical pattern of narrative development independently of any construction or interpretation. One must in addition engage – to repeat – in some sort of construal of one's life. One must have some sort of relatively large-scale coherence-seeking, unity-seeking, pattern-seeking, or most generally

[F] *form-finding* tendency

when it comes to one's apprehension of one's life, or relatively large-scale parts of one's life.[28]

---

[27] MacIntyre does not in the passages I have quoted explicitly say that the narrativity of a life requires Narrativity. In *After Virtue* he is particularly concerned with the idea that 'to think of a human life as a narrative unity is to think in a way alien to the dominant individualist and bureaucratic modes of modern culture' (1981, p. 211), and this remark was principally a criticism – an excellent one – of the social sciences of the time.

[28] From now on I will omit the qualification about 'parts of one's life' and take it as read.

– But this doesn't even distinguish Narrativity from Diachronicity, for to be Diachronic is already to put a certain construction on one's life – on the life of the human being that one is: it is to apprehend that life through the life-unifying sense that one(*) was there in the past and will be there in the future. And yet you say being Diachronic is not enough for being Narrative.

I'm prepared to allow that to be Diachronic is already to put a certain construction on one's life in the sense you specify. Nevertheless one can be Diachronic without actively conceiving of one's life, consciously or unconsciously, as some sort of ethical-historical-characterological developmental unity, or in terms of a story, a *Bildung* or 'quest'. One can be Diachronic without one's sense of who or what one is having any significant sort of *narrative* structure. And one can be Diachronic without one's apprehension of oneself as something that persists in time having any great importance for one.[29]

– You've already said that, and the question remains unanswered: what sort of construal is required for Narrativity? When does one cross the line from mere Diachronicity to Narrativity? This is still luminously unclear.

I agree that the proposal that form-finding is a necessary condition of Narrativity is very unspecific, but its lack of specificity may be part of its value, and it seems clear to me that Diachronicity (D) and form-finding (F) are independent of each other. In practice, no doubt, they often come together, but one can imagine [–D +F] an Episodic person in whom a form-finding tendency is stimulated precisely by lack of a Diachronic outlook, and, conversely, [+D –F] a Diachronic person who lives, by force of circumstance, an intensely picaresque and disjointed life, while having absolutely no tendency to seek unity or narrative-developmental pattern in it. Other Diachronics in similar circumstances may move from [+D –F] to [+D +F], acquiring a form-finding tendency precisely because they become distressed by the 'one damned thing after another'[30] character of their lives. The great and radically non-Narrative Stendhal might be judged to be an example of this, in the light of all his chaotic autobiographical projects, although I would be more inclined to classify

---

[29] 'Discern', 'apprehend', 'find', 'detect' all have non-factive readings.
[30] Hubbard 1909, p. 32.

him as [−D +F].[31] Either way, the fact remains that one can be Diachronic while being very unreflective about oneself. One can be inclined to think, of any event in one's past of which one is reminded, that it happened to oneself*, without positively grasping one's life as a unity in any further – e.g. specifically narrative – sense.

I think that the notion of form-finding captures something that is essential to being Narrative and that goes essentially beyond being Diachronic, and one view might be that form-finding is not only necessary for Narrativity, but also minimally sufficient. Against that, it may be said that if one is genuinely Narrative one must also (and of course) have some sort of distinctive

[**S**] *story-telling* tendency

when it comes to one's apprehension of one's life – where story-telling is understood in such a way that it does not imply any tendency to fabrication, conscious or otherwise, although it does not exclude it either. On this view, one must be disposed to apprehend or think of oneself and one's life as fitting the form of some recognized narrative genre.

Story-telling is a species of form-finding, and the basic model for it, perhaps, is the way in which gifted and impartial journalists or historians report a sequence of events. Obviously they select among the facts, but they do not, we suppose, distort or falsify them, and they do more than merely list them in the correct temporal order, for they also place them in a connected account. In its non-falsifying mode story-telling involves the ability to detect – not invent – developmental coherencies in the manifold of one's life. It is one way in which one may be able to apprehend the deep personal constancies that do in fact exist in the life of every human being – although I believe this can also be done by form-finding without story-telling.

So story-telling entails form-finding, and story-telling in addition to form-finding is surely – trivially – sufficient for Narrativity.

8 A third and more troubling suggestion is that if one is Narrative one will also have a tendency to engage unconsciously in invention, fiction of some sort – falsification, confabulation, revi-

---

[31] I judge Stendhal to be strongly Episodic but subject to Diachronic flashes. Jack Kerouac is I think a case of an Episodic looking for larger form. There are also clear elements of this in Malcolm Lowry.

sionism – when it comes to one's apprehension of one's own life. I will call this

[**R**] revision.

According to *the revision thesis* Narrativity always carries with it some sort of tendency to revision, where revision essentially involves more merely than changing one's view of the facts of one's life. (One can change one's view of the facts of one's life without any falsification, simply by coming to see things more clearly.)

Revision in the present sense is by definition non-conscious. It may sometimes begin consciously, with deliberate lies told to others, for example, and it may have semi-conscious instars, but it is not genuine revision in the present sense unless or until its products are felt to be true in a way that excludes awareness of falsification.[32] The conscious/non-conscious border is both murky and porous, but I think the notion of revision is robust for all that. The paradigm cases are clear, and extremely common.

If the revision thesis were true, it would be bad news for the ethical Narrativity thesis, whose supporters cannot want ethical success to depend essentially on some sort of falsification. I have no doubt that almost all human Narrativity is compromised by revision, but I don't think it must be. It is in any case a vast and complex phenomenon, and I will make just a very few remarks.

It is often said that autobiographical memory is an essentially *constructive* and *reconstructive* phenomenon (in the terms of experimental psychology) rather than a merely *reproductive* one, and there is a clear sense in which this is true.[33] Memory deletes, abridges, edits, reorders, italicizes. But even if construction and reconstruction are universal in autobiographical memory, they needn't involve revision as currently defined, for they may be fabrication-free story-telling or form-finding. Many have proposed that we are all without exception incorrigible self-fabulists, 'unreliable narrators' of our own lives,[34] and some who hold this view

---

[32] It's well known that fully conscious lies can forget their origins and come to be fully believed by their perpetrators.

[33] For good discussions, see e.g. Brewer 1988, McCauley 1988.

[34] Cf. e.g. Bruner 1987, 1990, 1994. The notion of an 'unreliable narrator' derives from literary criticism. In *The Minds' Past* (1998a) Gazzaniga seems to support a strongly reconstructive view of human memory, but he later says only that personal memory tends to be 'a bit fictional' (1998b, p. 713).

claim greater honesty of outlook for themselves, and see pride, self-blindness, and so on in those who deny it. But other research makes it pretty clear that this is not true. It's not true of everyone. We have here another deep dimension of human psychological difference. Some people are fabulists all the way down. In others, autobiographical memory is fundamentally non-distorting, whatever automatic processes of remoulding and recasting it may invariably involve.[35]

Some think that revision is always *charged*, as I will say – always motivated by an interconnected core group of moral emotions including pride, self-love, conceit, shame, regret, remorse, and guilt. Some go further, claiming with Nietzsche that we always revise in our own favour: ' "I have done that", says my memory. "I cannot have done that", says my pride, and remains inexorable. Eventually – memory yields.'[36]

It seems, however, that neither of these claims is true. The first, that all revision is charged, is significantly improved by the inclusion of things like modesty or low self-esteem, gratitude or forgiveness, in the core group of motivating moods and emotions; some people are just as likely to revise to their own detriment and to others' advantage as the other way round. But the claim that revision is always charged remains false even so. Revision may occur simply because one is a natural form-finder but a very forgetful one and instinctively seeks to make a coherent story out of limited materials.[37] Frustrated story-tellers may fall into revision simply because they can't find satisfying form in their lives and without being in any way motivated by a wish to preserve or restore self-respect. John Dean's recall of his conversations with Nixon at the Watergate hearings is another much discussed case of uncharged revision. When the missing tapes were found, his testimony was revealed to be impressively 'accurate about the individuals' basic positions' although it was 'inaccurate with respect to exactly what was said during a given conversation'. His recall of events involved revision in addition to routine forgetting and morally neutral reconstruction, in so far as it contained positive

---

[35] Brewer (1988) argues that the evidence that supports 'the reconstructive view of personal memory . . . does not seem very compelling'. See also Wagenaar 1994, Baddeley 1994, p. 239, Swann 1990. Ross (1989) argues that revision that seems to serve self-esteem may be motivated by nothing more than a concern for consistency.

[36] 1886, §69.

[37] Perhaps 'confabulation' in patients with Korsakov's syndrome is an extreme and pathological example of revision. See e.g. Sacks 1985, Gazzaniga 1998.

mistakes, but there is no reason to think that it was significantly charged.[38] 'Flashbulb' memories (such as the memory of what was one doing when one heard about the shooting of President Kennedy or about 9/11) can be surprisingly inaccurate – astonishingly so given our certainty that we remember accurately – but once again there seems no reason to think that the revision that they involve must be charged.[39]

Even when revision is charged, the common view that we always revise in our own favour must yield to a mass of everyday evidence that some people are as likely to revise to their own detriment – or simply forget the good things they have done.[40] When La Rochefoucauld says that self-love is subtler than the subtlest man in the world, there is truth in what he says. And revising to one's own detriment may be no more attractive than revising to one's advantage. But La Rochefoucauld is sometimes too clever, or rather ignorant, in his cynicism.[41]

Is a tendency to revise a necessary part of being Narrative? No. In our own frail case, substantial Narrativity may rarely occur without revision, but story-telling is sufficient for Narrativity, and one can be story-telling without being revisionary. So the ethical Narrativity thesis survives the threat posed by the revision thesis. When Bernard Malamud claims that 'all biography is ultimately fiction', simply on the grounds that 'there is no life that can be captured wholly, as it was', there is no implication that it must also be ultimately untrue.[42]

9 I've made some distinctions, but none of them cut very sharply, and if one asks how Diachronics, form-finders, story-tellers, and revisers relate to each other, the answer, as far as I can see, is that almost anything goes. Story-telling entails form-finding because it is simply one kind of form-finding, but I see no other necessary connections between the four. Some think that all normal human beings have all four of these properties. I think that some normal human beings have none of them. Some think that Narrativity

---

[38] Brewer 1988, p. 27. Cf. Neisser 1981.
[39] Pillemer 1998, ch. 2.
[40] For more formal evidence, cf. e.g. Wagenaar 1994, 'Is memory self-serving?'.
[41] Even if we did all tend to see our lives in a favourable light, it would not follow that we were all revisers: some will have self-favouring, self-respect-preserving justifications of their actions already in place at the time of action, and so have no need for subsequent revision.
[42] Malamud 1979.

necessarily involves all four. I think (as just remarked) that the limiting case of Narrativity involves nothing more than form-finding story-telling (it does not even require one to be Diachronic).

How do the authors I've quoted classify under this scheme? Well, Dennett is someone who endorses a full blown [+D +F +S +R] view of what it is to be Narrative, and he seems to place considerable emphasis on revision:

> our fundamental tactic of self-protection, self-control, and self-definition is not spinning webs or building dams, but telling stories, and more particularly *concocting* and controlling the story we tell others – and ourselves – about who we are.[43]

Bruner, I think, concurs with this emphasis. I take it that Sartre endorses [+F +S +R], and is not particularly concerned with [D] in so far as he is mainly interested in short-term, in-the-present story-telling. Schechtman's account of Narrativity is [+D +F +S ±R]. It assumes that we are all Diachronic, requires that we be form-finding and story-telling and explicitly so:

> constituting an identity requires that an individual conceive of his life as having the form and the logic of a story – more specifically, the story of a person's life – where "story" is understood as a conventional, linear narrative[44]

but it is important, on her view, that there be no significant revision, that one's self-narrative be essentially accurate.

I take myself to be [−D −F −S −R]. The claim that I don't revise much is the most vulnerable one, because it is in the nature of the case that one has no sense that one revises when one does. So I may be wrong, but (of course) I don't think so.

On the strong form of Schechtman's view, I am not really a person. Some sentient creatures, she says 'weave stories of their lives, and it is their doing so which *makes* them persons'; to have an 'identity' as a person is 'to have a narrative self-conception . . . to experience the events in one's life as interpreted through one's sense of one's own life story'. This is in fact a common type

---

[43] 1991, p. 418; my emphasis. Note that Dennett stresses the idea that this is a story about who we are, rather than about our lives.

[44] Schechtman 1997, p. 96. This is a strong expression of her view, which has usefully weaker forms (cf. e.g. pp. 117, 159).

of claim, and Schechtman goes further, claiming at one point that 'elements of a person's narrative' that figure only in his 'implicit self-narrative', and that 'he cannot articulate . . . are only partially his – attributable to him to a lesser degree than those aspects of the narrative he can articulate'.[45]

This seems to me to express an ideal of control and self-awareness in human life that is mistaken and potentially pernicious. The aspiration to explicit Narrative self-articulation is natural for some – for some, perhaps, it may even be helpful – but in others it is highly unnatural and ruinous. My guess is that it almost always does more harm than good – that the Narrative tendency to look for story or narrative coherence in one's life is, in general, a gross hindrance to self-understanding: to a just, general, practically real sense, implicit or explicit, of one's nature. It's well known that telling and retelling one's past leads to changes, smoothings, enhancements, shifts away from the facts, and recent research has shown that this is not just a human psychological foible. It turns out to be an inevitable consequence of the mechanics of the neurophysiological process of laying down memories that every studied conscious recall of past events brings an alteration.[46] The implication is plain: the more you recall, retell, narrate yourself, the further you risk moving away from accurate self-understanding, from the truth of your being. Some are constantly telling their daily experiences to others in a storying way and with great gusto. They are drifting ever further off the truth. Others never do this, and when they are obliged to convey facts about their lives they do it clumsily and uncomfortably and in a way that is somehow essentially narrative-resistant.

Certainly Narrativity is not a necessary part of the 'examined life' (nor is Diachronicity), and it is in any case most unclear that the examined life, thought by Socrates to be essential to human existence, is always a good thing. People can develop and deepen in valuable ways without any sort of explicit, specifically Narrative reflection, just as musicians can improve by practice sessions without recalling those sessions. The business of living well is, for many, a completely non-Narrative project. Granted that certain sorts of self-understanding are necessary for a good human life, they need involve nothing more than form-finding, which can

[45] 1997, p. 117.
[46] See McCrone 2003, Debiec, LeDoux, & Nader 2002.

exist in the absence of Narrativity; and they may be osmotic, systemic, not staged in consciousness.

Psychotherapy need not be a narrative or Narrative project. It regularly involves identifying connections between features of one's very early life and one's present perspective on things, but these particular explanatory linkings need not have any sort of distinctively narrative character to them. Nor need they be grasped in any distinctively Narrative way. Nor need they interconnect narratively with each other in any interesting way. I don't need to take up any sort of Narrative attitude to myself in order to profit from coming to understand how the way X and Y treated me when I was very young is expressed in certain anxieties I have now. The key explanatory linkings in psychotherapy are often piecemeal in nature, as are many of the key impacts of experience. Ideally, I think, one acquires an assorted basketful of understandings, not a narrative – an almost inevitably falsifying narrative.

10 – *I'm sorry, but you really have no idea of the force and reach of the psychological Narrativity thesis. You're as Narrative as anyone else, and your narratives about yourself determine how you think of yourself even though they are not conscious.*

Well, here we have a stand off. I think it's just not so, and I take it that the disagreement is not just terminological. Self-understanding does not have to take a narrative form, even implicitly. I'm a product of my past, including my very early past, in many profoundly important respects. But it simply does not follow that self-understanding, or the best kind of self-understanding, must take a narrative form, or indeed a historical form. If I were charged to make my self-understanding explicit, I might well illustrate my view of myself by reference to things I (GS) have done, but it certainly would not follow that I had a Diachronic outlook, still less a Narrative one.

At this point Heidegger informs us, in a variation on Socrates, that a human being's existence – 'Dasein's' existence – is constituted by the fact that its being is an issue for it. Fine, but it's not at all clear that being a thing whose being is an issue for it need involve any sort of Narrative outlook. Heidegger takes it that one's 'self-understanding is constitutive of [one's] . . . being what or who [one] is', and that this self-understanding consists largely in one's 'determining oneself as someone by pressing ahead into a possible way to be'.[47] And here he seems (I do not understand his notion of temporality) to be insisting on the importance of being Diachronic and indeed Narrative. But if this is his claim then – once again – it seems to me false: false as a universal claim about human life, false as a claim about what it is for human beings to be what or who they are, false as a normative claim about what good or authentic human life must be like, false about what any self-understanding must involve, and false about what self-understanding is at its best. Perhaps Heideggerian authenticity is compatible with the seemingly rival ideal of living in the moment – 'Take therefore no thought for the morrow: for the morrow shall take thought for the things of itself. Sufficient unto the day is the evil thereof'[48] – but this will not win me over.

11 There is much more to say. Some may still think that the Episodic life must be deprived in some way, but truly happy-go-lucky, see-what-comes-along lives are among the best there are, vivid, blessed, profound.[49] Some think that an Episodic cannot really know true friendship, or even be loyal. They are refuted by Michel de Montaigne, a great Episodic, famous for his friendship with Etienne de la Boétie, who judged that he was 'better at friendship than at anything else' although

> there is nobody less suited than I am to start talking about memory. I can find hardly a trace of it in myself; I doubt if there is any other memory in the world as grotesquely faulty as mine is![50]

Montaigne finds that he is often misjudged and misunderstood, for when he admits he has a very poor memory people assume that he must suffer from ingratitude: 'they judge my affection by my memory', he comments, and are of course quite wrong to do so.[51] A gift for friendship doesn't require any ability to recall past

---

[47] Blattner 1999, pp. 32, 41; I substitute 'one' for 'Dasein'. Cf. Heidegger (1927, p. 344): 'In the light of the "for-the-sake-of-which" of one's self-chosen ability-to-be, resolute Dasein frees itself for its world.'

[48] *Matthew* vi. 34. This way of being in the present has nothing to do with the 'aesthetic' way of being in the present described and condemned by Kierkegaard.

[49] Note, though, how Tom Bombadil in *The Lord of the Rings* can produce a certain anxiety.

[50] 1563–92, p. 32.

[51] p. 33. 'A second avantage' of poor memory, he goes on to note, 'is that . . . I remember less any insults received'.

shared experiences in detail, nor any tendency to value them. It is shown in how one is in the present.

But can Episodics be properly moral beings? The question troubles many. Kathy Wilkes thinks not.[52] So also, perhaps, do Plutarch and many others. But Diachronicity is not a necessary condition of a properly moral existence, nor of a proper sense of responsibility.[53] As for Narrativity, it is in the sphere of ethics more of an affliction or a bad habit than a prerequisite of a good life. It risks a strange commodification of life and time – of soul, understood in a strictly secular sense. It misses the point. 'We live', as the great short story writer V. S. Pritchett observes, 'beyond any tale that we happen to enact'.[54]

References

Baddeley, A. (1994). 'The remembered self and the enacted self', in *The remembering self: construction and accuracy in the self-narrative*, edited by U. Neisser & R. Fivush (Cambridge: Cambridge University Press).

Blattner, W. (1999). *Heidegger's Temporal Idealism* (Cambridge: Cambridge University Press).

Blumenfeld, L. (2003). *Revenge: a Story of Hope* (New York: Washington Square Press).

Brewer, W. F. (1988). 'Memory for randomly sampled autobiographical events', in *Remembering Reconsidered: Ecological and traditional approaches to the study of memory* edited by U. Neisser & E. Winograd (Cambridge: Cambridge University Press).

Bruner, J.. (1987). 'Life as Narrative', *Social Research* 54, pp. 11–32.

——. (1990). *Acts of Meaning* (Cambridge, MA: Harvard University Press).

——. (1994). 'The "remembered" self', in *The remembering self*.

Campbell, J. (1994). *Past, Space, and Self* (Cambridge, MA: MIT Press).

Debiec, J., LeDoux, J. and Nader, K. (2002). 'Cellular and Systems Reconsolidation in the Hippocampus' *Neuron* 36(3), pp. 527–538.

Dennett, D. (1988). 'Why everyone is a novelist' *Times Literary Supplement* 16–22 September.

Gazzaniga, M. (1998a). *The Mind's Past* (Berkeley: University of California Press).

——. (1998b). 'The Neural Platonist', *Journal of Consciousness Studies* 5, pp. 706–717, also at *http://www.imprint.co.uk/gazza_iv.htm*.

Heidegger, M. (1927/1962). *Being and Time*, translated by J. MacQuarrie & E. Robinson (Oxford: Blackwell).

Hirst, W. (1994). 'The remembered self in amnesics', in *The remembering self*.

Hubbard, E. (1909). article in *Philistine*.

James, H. (1864–1915/1999). *Henry James: a Life in Letters*, edited by Philip Horne (London: Penguin).

McCauley, R. N. (1988). 'Walking in our own footsteps: Autobiographical memory and reconstruction' in *Remembering Reconsidered*.

McCrone, J. (2003). *New Scientist*, May 3.

---

[52] Wilkes 1999.

[53] I discuss Episodic ethics in *Life in Time*.

[54] Pritchett 1979, p. 47. I am grateful to audiences in Oxford (1999), Rutgers (2000), and Reading (2003) for their comments.

MacIntyre, A. (1981). *After Virtue* (London: Duckworth).

Malamud, B. (1979). *Dubin's Lives* (New York: Farrar Straus & Giroux).

Montaigne, M. de (1563–92/1991). *The Complete Essays*, translated by M. A. Screech (London: Penguin).

Neisser, U. (1981). 'John Dean's memory: A case study' in *Cognition* 9, pp. 1–22.

Pillemer, D. (1998). *Momentous Events, Vivid Memories: How Unforgettable Moments Help Us Understand the Meaning of Our Lives* Cambridge, MA: Harvard University Press.

Plutarch, (c 100 AD/1939). 'On Tranquillity of Mind' in Plutarch, *Moralia* VI, translated by W. C. Helmbold (Cambridge, MA: Harvard University Press).

Ross, M. (1989). 'Relation of implicit theories to the construction of personal histories' *Psychological Review* 96, pp. 341–357.

Sacks, O. (1985). *The Man Who Mistook His Wife For A Hat* (London: Duckworth).

Sartre, J.-P. (1938/1996). *La nausée* (Paris: Gallimard).

Schechtman, M. (1997). *The Constitution of Selves* (Ithaca: Cornell University Press).

Scoville, W. B. and Milner, B. (1957). 'Loss of recent memory after bilateral hippocampal lesions', *Journal of Neurology, Neurosurgery, and Psychiatry* **20**, pp. 11–21.

Shaftesbury, Earl of (1698–1712/1900). 'Philosophical Regimen', in *The Life, Unpublished Letters, and Philosophical Regimen of Anthony, Earl of Shaftesbury*, edited by B. Rand (New York: Macmillan).

Strawson, G. (1997). ' "The Self" ', in *Models of the Self* ed. S. Gallagher & J. Shear (Thorverton: Imprint Academic), pp. 1–24, also at *http://www.imprint.co.uk/strawson.htm.*

——. (1999). 'The Self and the SESMET', in *Models of the Self*, pp. 483–518, also at *http://www.imprint.co.uk/pdf/sesmet.pdf.*

——. (in preparation). *Life in Time* (Oxford: Oxford University Press).

Swann, W. B. (1990). 'To be adored or to be known: the interplay of self-enhancement and self-verification' in *Handbook of motivation and cognition: Foundations of social behavior*, edited by R. M. Sorrentino, & E. T. Higgins, volume 2 (New York: Guilford).

Taylor, C. (1989). *Sources of the Self* (Cambridge: Cambridge University Press).

Wagenaar, W. (1994). 'Is memory self-serving?', in *The remembering self.*

Wilkes, K. (1998). 'GNOTHE SEAUTON (Know Thyself)', *Journal of Consciousness Studies* 5, pp. 153–65 reprinted in *Models of the Self.*

CHAPTER 5

TRANSCENDENCE OF THE EGO
(THE NON-EXISTENT KNIGHT)

Bas C. van Fraassen

I am as inseparable from the world as light, and yet exiled as light is, gliding over the surface of stones and water, never gripped nor held.[1]

I exist, but I am not a thing among things. I am neither a physical object nor a mental substance or abstract entity, nor a compound thereof. I am not animal, mineral, or vegetable. Nor am I a thing constituted by or composed of things of that sort taken together. I am not some piece of furniture of the universe.

Certainly I have a body and I have thoughts as well as feelings. I have a spatial location as well as a place, however modest, in history. But I am not to be identified with any of this.[2] I am in this world, but not of this world. I am not a thing among things.

Logic: I exist

The view just expressed is logically coherent. Despite my leading quotation from Sartre, my own usage of 'exists' is not that of the Existentialists. Accepting the ground rules of Quine's 'On what there is', I equate '. . . exists' with 'There is such a thing as . . .'. Pegasus exists if and only if there is such a thing as Pegasus.

How can I say then that I exist, hence that there is such a thing as me, but also I am not a thing? There is an ambiguity in the English language. In such 'quantifier' locutions as 'something' or 'there is such a thing as' or 'everything', the word 'thing' does not occur with any substantive meaning, but is a sort of pronomial device. In elementary logic we paraphrase 'Something is

---

[1] 'Aussi inséparable du monde que la lumière et pourtant exilé, comme la lumière, glissant à la surface des pierres et de l'eau, sans que rien, jamais, ne m'accroche ou ne m'ensable.' Jean-Paul Sartre, *Le Sursis*. Paris: Gallimard 1945. From the Chapter '*Mardi 27 Septembre*'.

[2] Ingmar Persson's 'Self-Doubt: Why We Are Not Identical To Things Of Any Kind' signals agreement in its title, though in ways that I still need to explore.

. . .' as 'There is an x such that x . . .' For example, 'Everything beautiful is good' we render as '(All x)(if x is beautiful then x is good)'. The word 'thing' has disappeared. The example's logical structure is displayed in the paraphrase 'Everything is such that if it is beautiful then it is good'. Two of the three occurrences of 'x' correspond therefore to the relative pronoun 'it'. But the first occurrence of 'x', corresponding to the 'thing' part of 'Everything', does not play a different role from the others.[3] In venerable terminology, its use is not categorematic but syncategorematic.[4]

'Thing' and 'object'

When I say that I am not a thing, not an object, I mean this in the more substantive senses of 'thing' and 'object' in which they are genuine common nouns.

I am not an object.

The self is not an object.

The word 'I' does not, on any proper occasion of use, refer to an object.

Physical events and processes as well as persistent, enduring materials count as objects. So do mental substances and mathematical objects, witches and demons, quantum fields and quarks, spacetime *pace* the substantivalists, other possible worlds on at least one conception thereof – always assuming that there are any. Is there anything at all besides objects? Yes: Selves, among other things (once again using 'things' syncategorematically).

My topic is the Self; but I equate 'What is the Self?' with the question 'What am I?'. I take the former to be but a quasi-impersonal way of posing a mystery that can in the last recourse only be expressed in first-person, indexical language.[5] So here is my first assumption: I refer to my self when I say 'I', and you refer

---

[3]   Clearer in combinatory logic: a universally quantified sentence says that a certain predicate has universal application.

[4]   In model theory the domain of a quantifier is a set; but nothing implies that it is a set of objects. Note moreover that since each model has a set as its domain, and there is no set that contains everything there is (on pain of contradiction), it follows that the meaning of 'for all x, . . .' as provided by a model is never 'for everything there is'. If in fact there is a set of all *objects*, or of all *things*, or of all *substances*, it also follows that 'everything' does not mean 'all objects', 'all things', or 'all substances'.

[5]   I must here leave aside how first-person, indexical expression differs from 'objective' description.

to your self when you say 'I'. For I take it that I refer to my self when and only when I refer to myself.

That my self is the referent of my word 'I' is not a necessary assumption. Galen Strawson does not accept this, and says from the outset that the self is not the whole person.[6] In this he is in accord with much of modern philosophy, and I am not. But I take it that on all accounts, the question 'What am I?' – to which I limit myself – is crucially pertinent to this subject of the Self.

My second assumption: most things we ordinarily say about ourselves are true. For example, I was in Princeton in March and in Oxford in May. Therefore I am a continuant, in the simple and ordinary sense that I existed throughout at least some stretch of time.

The no-self view

On one view the putatively referential use of 'I' creates a grammatical illusion. We recall Lichtenberg's critique of Descartes' *Cogito*: there is thinking going on, but it does not follow that there is something that thinks. The view that there isn't anything at all that thinks I'll call the No-Self view. I do not subscribe to it, for I insist that although *the self is not some thing*, nevertheless *it is not nothing*.

Hume was certainly right that looking within oneself, one does not find any such *object* as the self or as his mind. This thinking *thing* (whatever it was that Descartes maintained we know better and more clearly than anything else) is not findable by introspection. Good point. Such phenomenological reflection however, if carried further, refutes identification of the self *with any recognizable object at all*. Introspecting I notice only my thoughts, my feelings, . . . , not the putative entity whose thoughts or feelings they are.[7] But this applies to my hands and feet as well. Here is Sartre's protagonist Matthieu in *Le Sursis*:

> He extended his hands and moved them slowly along the stone balustrade. . . . But just because he could see them they were

[6]   On Galen Strawson's view the question 'what is the self?' is distinct from 'what am I?'. I rely here on an unpublished lecture at Princeton University as well as his 'The Self', *J. Consciousness Studies* 4 (1997) 405–428.

[7]   Resist the temptation to postulate an object truly there but inaccessible to such reflection, as 'substratum' for what does appear. The self *transcends* all such appearances but that does not imply that the self is a *transcendent object*.

not his own, they were someone else's hands, they were outside,
like the trees, like the reflections on the Seine, hands that were
cut off.[8]

This is a universally recognizable experience: when we focus on
the hands as objects – as when we focus on our thoughts – they
become foreign objects.[9]

The underlying point here, about the form that experience can
take, is disputed by Quassim Cassam in his *Self and World*.[10] He
argues for a 'materialist conception of self-consciousness' in the
following form:

> our awareness of ourselves is a matter of one's being sensibly
> or intuitively aware of oneself qua subject as a physical object

Cassam's argument is ostensibly phenomenological; in fact, it
accepts a menu of traditional options, which he eliminates
one by one until only that conclusion remains. His argument
actually pays scant attention to the phenomenology of experience. That we experience ourselves as incarnate, as involved
in nature, is a far cry from that materialist conception of self-
consciousness.[11]

Incoherence of the no-self view

Whatever meta-linguistic dress we put on the No-Self view, it
appears to imply that I do not exist. But I do exist! Can this osten-
sible contradiction be finessed? The options are just two: to rein-
terpret the thesis about 'I', or to reconstrue 'I exist' as deceptive
in its grammatical form.

Call the latter option *Version One* of the No-Self view: there is
something drastically wrong with our way of speaking and think-

---

[8]   'Il étendit les mains et les promena lentement sur la pierre de la balustrade. . . . Mais,
justement parce qu'il pouvait les regarder, elles n'étaient plus à lui, c'étaient les mains
d'un autre, dehors, comme les arbres, comme les reflets qui tremblaient dans la Seine,
des mains coupées.' Sartre, *Le Sursis*, ibid.; p. 296.

[9]   If they are mine, *where* is the *me* whose they are? However, this experience does not
push us inexorably or logically toward the view that there is no me after all, as if there
were only my thoughts, hands, feelings, and so forth, travelling together like a small circus
troupe. Experience is neither the warrant for, nor the fruit of, metaphysical beliefs.

[10]   Quassim Cassam, *Self and World*. Oxford: Oxford University Press 1997.

[11]   I doubt the very intelligibility of this 'as . . . qua . . .' locution; but let this pass.

ing. When we say 'It rains', 'It thunders' or 'It snows' the word 'it', though grammatically the subject term, does not have a referent. By analogy, the surface subject-predicate form of 'I am thinking' may be deceptive.

This version is actually just a promissory note that we have no way of cashing in.

(a) When thinking is going on, is it also the case that there is nothing that is thinking?

Judging by the surface grammar, 'Nothing is thinking' appears to contradict 'I am thinking'. The difference is that in the case of 'It rains' we can add an explanation whose surface grammar is not deceptive – about humid air and condensation. Therefore to press the analogy is to invite a similar completion, and what are the options there? Materialist or dualist stories about how there is thinking going on. But such a completion entirely defeats the charm and appeal of the 'grammatical illusion' move.

(b) How do we distinguish 'I am thinking' from 'You are thinking', since in both cases thinking is going on?

In the case of rain, we can say of course that it is raining in Princeton and not in Oxford. Again, the analogy invites some completion, to locate the thinking in various places, bodies, minds, or the like; and we may enter the same comment as before.

(c) How do we construe 'I exist now, but did not exist before 1900'?

The example of thinking, natural enough when confronting Descartes, is rather special. If the No-Self view is to be taken seriously it must extend to other uses of 'I'. In this example, I convey the information that the person BvF has existed only after 1900. So the most natural construal is that 'I' does have a referent, namely that person. Why here and not everywhere else?

Version Two reconstrues the thesis that 'I' is not a referring term to: its uses do not ever refer to an object. I am not an object of any sort. But that allows us to add that my use of 'I' does refer, namely to me – who am not an object.

Identification: I am not a thing

Why am I not the most obvious thing that people see when they look at me – namely my body?

My reason for this denial is the unforgiving, uncompromising Principle of the Excluded Middle. I do not insist that this principle holds with logical universality. But it holds for discourse about bodies and physical objects in general. If I am my body then there must be a fact of the matter as to which object in the world is my body. Once we test this presupposition it fades into thin air. There is an insightful dramatization of the options open to an advocate of body-self identity in a novel by Italo Calvino.[12]

The non-existent knight

Charlemagne is inspecting his arrayed knights before a military campaign against the Infidels. One knight on a white charger, in immaculately gleaming armor, has not raised his visor. Commanded to do so, he demurs; when he does raise it, there is nothing inside the armor. 'I do not exist', the knight explains. If he does not exist, how does he do his duty? 'By willpower and faith in our holy cause!' 'Oh yes, yes, well said, yes, that is how one does one's duty', the Emperor responds, a little thoughtfully.

This non-existent knight, Agilulf, has armor, a horse, a sword, habits of movement as well as of thought, though he has no body. What does he mean then, that he does not exist? Without accepting a general materialist position, one may hold that human existence is necessarily or essentially embodied. So if with the existentialists one reserves the term for human existence – then there is such a person as Agilulf but he does not *exist*.

The knight Agilulf (who has no body) and his squire Gurduloo (who cannot distinguish himself from his material surroundings) are the illuminating extremes:

> The only person who can be said to be definitely on the move is Agilulf, by which I do not mean his horse or armour, but that lonely self-preoccupied impatient something jogging along on horseback inside the armour. Around him pine cones fall from branches, streams gurgle over pebbles, fish swim in streams, . . . ; but all this is mere illusion of movement, perpetual revolv-

[12] Italo Calvino, *Il Cavaliere Inesistente*. Torino: Giulio Einaudi Editore S.p.A., 1959.; tr. Archibald Colquhoun in Italo Calvino, *Our Ancestors: The Cloven Viscount. The Baron in the Trees. The Non-Existent Knight*. New York: Vintage/Ebury, 1980.

ing to and fro like waves. And in this wave Gurduloo is revolving to and fro, prisoner of the material world, he too is smeared like the pine cones, fish, maggots, stones and leaves, a mere excrescence on the earth' crust.[13]

We, in contrast, are 'creatures of the middle', to echo Pascal. But the extremes illustrate aspects of the sort of existence I (and you reader, *mon semblable, mon frère, ma soeur*) can claim.

The Gurduloo problem

What in the world is my body? Where is the demarcation between that body and the rest of nature? We can consider ways of drawing the line by purely physical criteria, by phenomenology, by psychological factors, or by social construction.

When I think about the crucial importance of my body in the determination of what I am, I think first of all about how I express myself bodily, through posture and motion as well as speech, writing, and other manual labor. But I express myself also through my clothes, car, house, garden, . . . Should I not count these part of my body, in an extended sense, if I am to have a plausible sense for 'I am my body'? True, those are all detachable parts. But so are my hair and nails. True, I can change my clothes without endangering my identity; but so can I change my hair color and even skin color (at least from pinko-grey to bronze). True, I can exchange my house for another house and car for another car. But I can also have a cornea, kidney or heart transplant. Transplants of both sorts are only contingently easy or hard: under certain conceivable social and economic conditions, a heart transplant may be easier to achieve than a change of jeans.

The difficulty of distinguishing our bodily self from our physical environment is graphically portrayed by Gurduloo. We first see him paddling among a flock of ducks, quacking, 'the rags he wore, of earthen color . . . had big greenish-gray areas the same color as feathers'. (p. 24) Does he think he is a duck too? The girl whose ducks they are says No, he thinks the ducks are him. Eating soup, he ends up in the kettle, exclaiming 'All is soup'. (p. 53) An old peasant says 'He's just a person who exists and doesn't realize he exists'. (p. 28. Well, it was a French peasant.)

---

[13] Calvino, *Non-Existent Knight*, in Ch. 9.

Gurduloo is an extreme case, of the kind Harry Frankfurt calls 'wanton'.[14] He has no second order preferences that could sort out his immediate desires. Hence we can't read a sense of 'self-preservation' into his behavior. If we could, we would be seeing a privileged line of demarcation between his body and environment. That we cannot shows how such a demarcation is not, ever, independent of the importance of what matters to us. This makes for a problem for any attempt to identify oneself with one's body. If I am a physical object, then there is a fact of the matter as to which I am. What fact is that? How could it, without circularity, fail to be independent of what matters to me?

The difficulties in the demarcation of my body on a 'folk' level of discussion pale by comparison when the question is transposed to a scientific realist world picture. How are ordinary movable middle-sized objects to be identified in a world of quantum fields, for example? The quandaries we are in here are tellingly explored in Brian Smith's *On the Origin of Objects*.[15] Despairing of a purely 'objective' (physicalist) solution, one may try for a pragmatic solution, such as that *being an object* is a 'response-dependent' concept. One might elaborate the idea by saying, for instance, that the objects in this world are precisely our selective clumpings of bits of stuff as a function of our needs and interests. (This seems to be what Brian Smith favors.) But this cannnot be an option if I am asserted to be identical with one of those objects! The pragmatic turn loses us any remaining grip on the factual question 'Which object am I?'

Minimalist body-mind identifications

If the Gurduloo problem, of determining one's body among all the parts of nature, is insoluble in purely physical terms then we might look to other criteria: biological, medical, legal, psychological, phenomenological, social. I submit that these are either linked indissolubly to specific purposes (with the constraints dictated by special interests) or else intensify the Gurduloo problem.

---

[14] See his *The Importance of What We Care About*. Cambridge: Cambridge University Press, 1988.

[15] Brian Cantwell Smith, *The Origin of Objects*. Cambridge, MA: MIT Press, 1998.

The life sciences

My body: which object precisely is that? In the life sciences there has been need for a precise answer to this question.[16]

Such an animal as the human is topologically speaking a torus, since the gastro-intestinal tract is a pathway going all the way through. The surface of a torus divides a three-dimensional space precisely into two parts, one finite (interior) and one infinite (exterior). My body is precisely the interior of this torus, plus its boundary – the skin, to be precise. Of course the precision is only of a degree sufficient for the life sciences' purposes. Some conventions also need to be introduced: hair is largely outside the skin, but we can re-classify it as skin; nails too of course. Such conventional choices are also constrained by the purpose at hand.

Alternatively one may define the interior/exterior by sterility: 'outside the body' is any non-sterile area. This removes the outside surface of the skin, but also certain regions we tend to think of as 'inside'. A more serious ambiguity derives from the functioning body's active resistance to things that do not respond in certain ways, through its immune system. Daily lifelong administration of immunosuppressive drugs is part of the regimen of all transplant recipients. If the body does not reject the transplant or implant during this drug regimen, is the tolerated artifact at that time part of the body? It may be entirely in the interior of the torus, and entirely sterile – but the body originally recognized it as alien, and drugs were needed to depress the immune response.

. . .

Imagine that the philosophical answer *Yes: I am my body* is met with the response: *In that case you are the interior plus boundary of the above described torus, qualified as indicated in the amendments listed.* We cannot read this response as scientific support for the assertion as a factual claim. We can only read it as specifying what the assertion means if read as a sentence *in an idiolect created to serve certain professional purposes.*

Suppose however we took 'The body is [thus and so, such and such an object]', presented as a *factual claim* coming from the life sciences. We would then still have to ask 'Fine; but are they right?' There have been many false hypotheses that were once accepted in science. So this would not be an idle question. But it would be puzzling, for what it asks for does not seem to be a matter to

---

[16] Thanks to Carmen dell' Aversano for helpful discussion.

subject to experiment. An experiment could test whether the interior of this torus is everywhere sterile, but how could it test the hypothesis that the entire interior and/or the surface are part of the body?

Legal arguments (e.g. about whether preserved sperm should be buried with the donor when deceased, and limits on lap dancing) do not simply draw on the life sciences for demarcation of the body.[17] This underlines the purpose-relative character of the question.

The absolute minimum?

If I am wearing clothes, perhaps I can say: my body is everything that is inside my clothes. That leaves a little uncertainty about the head and hands sticking out. If I am wearing a space-suit, I can try 'everything inside the space suit'. But that includes air and moisture outside my skin. The presence of this air and moisture are crucial to my existence there, as much as my blood and lymph. By what criterion can we exclude the absolutely necessary life support system for the bodily functions from the body? Alternatively we can ask: if we allow for any and all forms of life support as equally legitimate, how much of me has to survive for me to survive? Eric Olson's *The Human Animal* argues that only the brain stem's existence is necessary (and as a matter of fact, also sufficient) for the survival of the same animal.[18] Does that give us the principled criterion for demarcating the self?

Consider the principle that I am whatever thing is such that its existence is both necessary and sufficient for my survival as the same animal. If Olson is right, this principle would then imply that I am my brainstem. (I am not attributing this conclusion to Olson.) That I am my brain stem is at least a possible extreme of the 'I am my body' variants. Here after all we have the engine of reason and the seat of the soul, according to some – is that not precisely enough? Leave aside how curiously and arbitrarily selective it is to ask what is necessary and/or sufficient for survival after

---

[17] I have only anecdotal evidence, and would appreciate references; see further Andrews, Lori B. and Dorothy Nelkin, *Body Bazaar: The Market For Human Tissue In The Biotechnology Age.* New York: Crown, 2001.

[18] *The Human Animal: Personal Identity Without Psychology.* Oxford: Oxford University Press, 1997. Thanks to Eleonore Stump; see further her challenging 'Non-Cartesian substance dualism and materialism without reductionism', *Faith and Philosophy* 12 (1995), 505–531.

first excluding conditions of life support from consideration. We cannot accept this principle while also taking the self to be the person that I am, for the candidates this principle sanctions just do not seem to qualify as persons.

The unforgiving excluded middle

Attempts to identify myself with my body are thus thoroughly stumped by the Gurduloo problem.

The problem at issue is not the vagueness of our concepts, whether ordinary or crafted for scientific and practical purposes. There are bodies in the sense of the life sciences. There are well-defined organisms to be studied in those sciences, from cells to entire ecosystems. The level of precision in definition suits the purpose at hand; no more is required. Nor is the problem Gurduloo's case raises a problem about vagueness in general. The contours of most bodies to which we freely refer are indeed vague: clouds, roads, seas, prairies, mountains, . . . Nevertheless, K2 is a specific mountain, although it is not a specific heap of earth and stones; and it is distinct from other mountains such as Mt. Etna or Mt. Everest. Even vague objects can be distinguished from each other. So if there is a general problem of vagueness, it does not remove the question before us. We can sensibly ask which of those vague objects I am. The Gurduloo problem is not which body is which, although that is pertinent, but

> How can I possibly *identify* myself with any part of nature, however defined, given that I can discern only differences of degree and delineations that shift and deform from one perceptual context to another?[19]

The Excluded Middle is very unforgiving. If there is a fact of the matter about whether I am a physical object or system, then I am at most one of these so demarcated objects, and not another, and the facts must settle the matter. *But what facts could settle it?*

A philosopher may be tempted to replace that question with 'Is there any non-arbitrary, principled way to make the selection?' These two questions are not at all the same! A non-arbitrary, principled distinction may just be one that appeals to certain indis-

---

[19] There may be no way to express this problem in any but first-person language. The essential indexical may well be at the heart of this entire discussion.

putable theoretical virtues. Then an ostensibly factual question is being settled on the basis of preference – however non-arbitrary – for certain kinds of theory. *That is not settling by facts alone.* The question is not 'Which object *is it best* to postulate to be my body, in the development of a *satisfactory* scientific or metaphysical theory?' That question may be answerable, but does not respond to our concern.[20]

Manifestation, not identity

. . . Agilulf, by which I do not mean his horse or armor, but that lonely self-preoccupied, impatient something jogging along on horseback inside the armor.[21]

While identity is a black-and-white sort of relationship (I am either identical with x or distinct from x), my relationship to any of the things I call mine is not. We find only graduated and nuanced relations between ourselves and the things that we call ours, whether physical, psychological, or social. A question such as 'which particular object is my body?' is eventually unanswerable precisely because of its questionable – arguably untenable – presupposition of uniqueness. Therefore we need a distinct relational concept, different from identity yet non-trivial, to characterize our incarnate existence.

How do I relate to my body?

I express and reveal myself through bodily features and movements: through my posture, my physical comportment, my way of walking, my 'body language', my interaction with my natural and social environment, and thereby with the other selves who express themselves in similarly incarnate form. I express and reveal myself not only through the flesh but also through my clothes, my style of dressing, whether I ride my bicycle sedately or hands-off, how

---

[20] Some disagree here, because they accept explanatory power, unification, and simplicity as a guide to warranted belief. For them it must follow that theories are likelier to be true if they have these humanly desirable characteristics. What, I ask myself, could account for that? What does nature care?

[21] Calvino, *Non-Existent Knight*, from Ch. 9.

I arrange my living space, by where I walk as much as by how I walk.

Some ways of expression are more direct and less mediated. While none suffices to identify me, there is also no possibility of existence devoid of all such self-expression.

There is no bare homunculus at the heart of this living, moving presence. So how shall we picture our own existence to ourselves?

Expression is possible only in a language, in a broad sense of 'language'. Body language has a movement vocabulary, and means of composition of movements that have meaning. But there cannot be such a thing as a private language: you have a language only if you are a member of a language-endowed community. That is therefore a pre-condition of the very possibility of self-expression. To this social aspect I will return below.[22]

'Ye shall be as gods'

Satan said to Eve 'Ye shall be as gods', deceiving her into wanting what she already had. In the continuum-relation between her self and her bodily environment she already transcends all that is given in experience. This goes for her as well as for the as-serpent-appearing demon.

Mythical depiction of gods, angels, and demons dramatizes the distance between being in the world and being an object, as well as their self-expression through diverse incarnate and natural appearances. Needing a nuanced relational term also for us, let us therefore adapt one from myth. I *manifest* myself in nature, through my body, my movements, my words, my decorating and clothing activities, my artistic endeavors and literary output, my passions and tantrums, . . .

Think about us in the way the myths depict the Homeric and Hindu Gods, as well as the lesser supernaturals in the religions of the Book. (Remember Leda and the swan, Krishna as charioteer in the Bhaghavid Gita, Shiva who appears in creation and destruction, Satan's minions who at their choice appear to us as incubi or succubi.) The gradation that replaces both self-body separation and self-body identification is then evident. I manifest myself through temporarily enduring parts of nature such as my torso

---

[22] Thanks to Isabelle Peschard for discussion of this point. See also Anthony Synnott, *The Body Social: Symbolism, Self, And Society*. London: Routledge, 1993.

and limbs, as well as through my habitual though inconstant appearance as clothed in certain materials or none at all, as walking rather than driving, and so forth.

My physical attributes

I have many physical attributes, such as mass, position, and velocity. I have these precisely because I have a body; more accurately: because I am embodied. Our ordinary way of speaking about this fact underlines two salient points. First of all I speak of my body in the same way I speak of my clothes, house, car, friends, as something that is *not me but mine*. Secondly, the fuzzy boundaries that characterize those objects characterize equally the transfer-attribution of their physical characteristics. What is my body mass when I have just eaten and not yet digested a large pizza? Does it include the small parts of pizza still in my mouth, if I am still chewing? And what is my precise position when I am moving, and my hair, scarf, and billowing sleeves are blowing in the wind? Thirdly, this verbal distancing slides very easily into metaphor. For that reason we can't make it the arbiter of truth. Literally, the eye does not see. The eye sees only in the sense that the eye reads, which is the sense in which the hand writes and the mouth speaks. These are derivative properties of the parts, deriving from the whole, with the relationship metaphorically raised into an identity. Turn the metaphor back on itself. The hand writes only in the sense that I write with my hand, but I am extended in the sense that I have limbs and the like which are extended.

Spatial location

If the relations between ourselves and the objects, events, and processes in the world admit of degrees then many questions about us will be subject to irremediable ambiguity.

Where am I? If I were identical with a specific physical object, that question would have a definite answer. But does it? Trying to identify my location, I naturally turn to the center of my sensory perspectives.[23] A famous psychological experiment in which the

---

[23] See Michael Kubovy, Ch. 9 'The psychology of egocenters' in his *The Psychology Of Perspective And Renaissance Art*. Cambridge: Cambridge University Press, 1986.

subject aligns sticks to point at himself confirms our intuitive response. That places me somewhere in my head, behind my eyes and between my ears. Immediately I follow Descartes in picturing myself as a small homunculus sucking its sensory life out of the pineal gland. But now I close my eyes, it is deep in the night with not a sound anywhere, I move around, I feel around me. Now my perceptual center is somewhere behind my hands, it is not inside my head, I am phenomenologically located somewhere close behind the touch of those hands.

Psychological experiments severely disturb the pictures that bewitch philosophy. Michael Kubovy's is simple and striking:

> If I trace a 'b' on the back of your head, you'll report that I wrote a b; if I trace the same character on your forehead, you'll probably perceive it as a d. It's as if you had a 'disembodied eye' behind your head reading the pattern traced. We are engaged in research . . . to discover the body's natural systems of coordinates.[24]

The 'causal order'

It may well be objected that I am on this view rather insubstantial. Precisely so. I am no substance, nor was meant to be. I am present, and I act, but am not an object entering into the interactions studied by the natural sciences. I may be said to do so derivatively; for I have a body – however circumscribed in a given context – which does enter into those interactions. The body and its physical interactions are the subject of physics and physiology; not so my actions.

Princess Elizabeth of Bohemia asked Descartes: *how does the mind interact with the body?* Descartes had no satisfactory answer, nor could he have. What should we answer her if she raises her question again, for our current account of the Self? Briefly: *there is no need for mechanisms of interaction* if I want to act, *precisely because I am not an object.* Neither forces and collisions between physical objects nor – if such there be – powers, potencies, or principalities to connect the abstract or occult with the physical,

---

[24] Kubovy, *ibid.* and http://www.virginia.edu/~mklab/skin.html. But 'natural coordinates'? The origin and orientation change in this case while the body's spatial configuration remains the same.

are pertinent. Not being an object, when I wish to act I just do it.

This may take a moment to assimilate. If I am not a physical object, how can I exert force on the ground, how can I be heavy enough to make a dent? How do I move my arm? What relation is there between my decision to move my arm and the contraction of the muscles that produces this movement?

On their most literal reading, these questions trade on the assumption that I am a body interacting in a bodily way. Bracketing that assumption, we see that such a question as 'How do I move my arm?' can legitimately be construed in only three ways.

a) The straightforward request addressed to the physiologist and physicist, to explain the bodily movement.

The scientist is to provide us with a theory or model, written or constructed within a given set of parameters, pertaining to the physical processes that take place when I move my arm.

b) The question *How do I move my arm?* in the sense evident from Agilulf's reply to Charlemagne.

Agilulf's answer, 'by willpower and faith in our holy cause' locates the question in the framework of 'person discourse', in the 'space of reasons'.

c) The request for instruction, to be shown how it is done.

After I had my leg in a cast for six weeks in 1995 I needed to relearn stepping down a stairway. Asking someone else 'how do you step down a stair?' might have helped. The obvious initial answer, *I just do it,* is certainly correct. But it needs to be supplemented with something more to focus my attention in a useful way.

There is no peculiarly philosophical question beyond these three, except for someone who takes a peculiarly philosophical position on the Self. Descartes could not have answered Princess Elizabeth in this way. For he had identified selves as immaterial substances, in a context with set categories of action and causation. These he had mainly inherited from the metaphysical tradition he had been at pains to dislodge in other respects, and was now asking for its due. But that is a while ago; why keep revisiting his predicaments?

Location in the social fabric

I have a location also in the social fabric, what Bradley called my Station and Its Duties. What I ought to do derives from what I am: a citizen, a lover, a son, a father, a teacher. So does *what I am*: despicable because bourgeois, admirable because bloodied yet unbowed, and so forth. That is my position in the world, in a somewhat different but no less important sense than that of spatial position.

I manifest myself in nature and in the social world. Of course this is possible only for an embodied being. The relationships that define my social position have a strong physical core: ancestry, place of birth, verbal acts of commitment. They are displayed in my body, however narrowly or broadly demarcated.[25] The physical embodiment enters every aspect of human existence.

Listen to the narrator of Ermanno Bencivenga's fable 'Io'.[26] Once I was just me, he says, but that made things very difficult when meeting people. The question would always come up: who was I? All I could say was 'I'm me'. These meetings never led to anything. So I chose a name for myself, quite at random: Giovanni Spadone. That made all the difference. 'Oh, Giovanni Spadone! so glad to meet you! and where are you from, what do you do, who are your parents . . . ?' Of course, if they had responded instead with 'And who is Giovanni Spadone?' I would have landed back in the same predicament. . . . But you know, they never do that. . . .

This moral so evident in the necessary birth of a social identity has its twin in the conditions of a social death, witnessed in the demise of Agilulf. When other knights brag about their glorious deeds, the glaring inaccuracies don't really matter – they are who they are anyway.[27] But for Agilulf there is no recourse beyond his history. A doubt about the deed for which he received his knighthood calls him – who and what he is – into question. He is truly defined by his station and its duties, as constituted in detail by his

---

[25] See Anthony Synnott, *The Body Social: Symbolism, Self, and Society.* London: Routledge, 1993.

[26] In his *La Filosofia In Trentadue Favole.* Milan: A. Mondadori, 1991.

[27] Calvino, *Non-Existent Knight,* Ch. 7. I resist the reading that the person must have a reality or substance that supports counterfactuals, the 'could' and 'could have' involved in what they claim to be. It seems sufficient that *they are what they will have been,* and what they will have been is still in the future, held jointly in their hands and the hands of fate.

history; there is nothing more to him. Sadly, when he finds this
doubt confirmed he wanders off alone, takes off his armor. Then
there is no longer any such thing as Agilulf; and perhaps there
never was. . . .

Pseudo-problems pertaining to the self

Almost everything to be said on the subject of what I am is prey
to readings that turn it into metaphysics. Princess Elizabeth's
question concerning volitional action invited such a reading
already. Let me try to prevent some more before they can take
hold.

The unobservable and I

In philosophy of science I take the empiricist view that accepting
a scientific theory does not require belief in the reality of any
unobservable entities it postulates. Taking this view of what science
is does not by itself imply disbelief in unobservable entities. But
what an uncomfortable tension, if someone agnostic about the
unobservables postulated in physics were then to profess to be an
unobservable entity himself!

Am I observable? Certainly I am; did you think I was invisible
or intangible? But I am visible and tangible only because I have
a body; my visibility and tangibility are derivative properties. This
reply may be challenged as follows:

[1] If I am distinct from a given entity, then I am observable
only if there is a way to observe me without observing that
entity.

[2] But observation is by the senses.

[3] Anything observed by the senses is identical with some
physical entity (thing, event, or process).

[4] Therefore I am observable only if I am identical with some
physical entity.

I have more faults to find with this reasoning than I can count! I
will skip the obvious ones.

It would be uncomfortable for an empiricist about science to
profess to be an unobservable entity. But 'entity' is another

synonym for 'object' or 'thing', and I am not one. It is indeed not true to say that I am observable, except in the sense that I have an observable body. But that is because such terms as 'observable' and its contraries classify *things* (including of course events, processes, all those object-like things). Attributes pertaining directly to certain kinds of objects can apply to me derivatively, but not in any other way. With this distinction made we can see how the argument trades on equivocation. Surely what is at issue is what is directly encountered in experience, in any reasonable sense. You do encounter me directly in experience; but that encounter has certain physical relations involving our bodies as a precondition.

The most important point, though, is one about our philosophical dialogue. There is no relevant direct parallel at all between our discussion of the self and the empiricist's controversy with the scientific realist. For this talk about the Self, remember, is just talk about myself and about yourself. Whether to be agnostic is a question that simply does not arise. You are not a postulated theoretical entity, introduced for reasons of theorizing or fitting evidence; and neither am I.

Reduction, no; but supervenience?

Twentieth century analytic philosophy sometimes looks like just a sustained attempt at a consistency proof for materialism (physicalism, naturalism . . .).[28] The most direct way to prove arithmetic consistent would be to reduce it to pure logic – as the logicists tried. Similarly the most direct way to prove the consistency of physicalism about thought, emotion, charm, and other such person-attributes would be to reduce all that to what is described in physics. I won't rehash the history that made us give up on both those simplistic ideas. But there remains the recently most popular position of 'supervenience without reduction!'.

Does everything true about me supervene on facts about physical objects and structures? My view, as expressed so far, may be

---

[28]   In logic or mathematics, when a consistency result is proved the next challenge is to develop alternatives. Given the consistency of Euclidean geometry, the challenge lies in non-Euclidean models. If ZF is consistent with the axiom of choice we want at once to know if there are models of ZF that violate the axiom. This attitude leads to the creation of new methods and strange structures, hence new understanding. A consistency result for materialism should similarly be philosophically exciting only if it reveals ways to create new strange, paradoxical, and esoteric *alternative* conceptions of what we are.

compatible with that; but it is not what I mean. I do not contradict it, but only because the entire game looks to me like a prime
example of what Carnap had in mind in his 'Pseudoproblems in
Philosophy'.

Supervenience is usually explained with a heavy dose of modal
metaphysics, to me of dubious intelligibility. But the concept of
supervenience between two sorts of discourse is intelligible. These
could be the language of physics and the part of our language in
which we use 'folk' psychological terms – 'person talk'. Abstractly,
consider two languages, Q-discourse and F-discourse. Let the
supervenience claim be:

[Supervenience] for anything X stated in F-discourse, if X is
true then the world could not be different in that respect unless
something formulated in Q-discourse were also different.

An intuitive example: I am currently thinking about dragons.
I could not be thinking differently at this moment unless
something physical (e.g. the state of my cortex) were different
as well. Rendered in terms of language, we construe this as: the
F-sentence 'I am thinking about dragons' could not be false
without some change in the truthvalues of the Q-sentences as
well.

Although I have used the subjunctive, this can be explicated
as follows. Both forms of discourse admit of many models
(intuitively, representing 'ways the world could be') and these
models can be combined into models for the two together only
in certain ways. For these combined models, what the above claim
asserts is this:

[Supervenience] there are no distinct combined models in
which a given F sentence has different truth values while all Q
sentences have the same truth values.

Suppose that the supervenience claim is correct.

It is easiest to think about this in terms of the maximal consistent sets of sentences within the given language (roughly, what
Carnap called 'state-descriptions', ignoring his restriction to
finite size). Such a set sums up all that is true in one given way
that things could be, to the extent formulable in that language.
Let these 'state-descriptions' of the Q language form the family
{Q(i): i in index set I}. Finally, let us write [S] for the set of
combined models that satisfy a given sentence S (of either
discourse).

Then if F is an F-sentence, there can be no combined models M and M′ such that F and Q(k) are true in M while F is false but Q(k) true in M′. Hence the set of models satisfying Q(k) must either lie entirely within the set of those satisfying F, or entirely outside that set. That is, [Q(k)] is either included in [F] or else disjoint from [F]. Since the state-descriptions jointly exhaust what can be true, any model that satisfies F must lie in one of the [Q(i)]. Putting these two points together, [F] is just the union of all the sets [Q(i)], with i in I, that are included in [F]. In our example that means that a 'personal discourse' sentence is just the 'disjunction' (in a suitably extended sense) of 'physical discourse' descriptions.

Let us display this argument graphically, with a diagram depicting a violation of the supervenience claim. (I am representing propositions by the sets of worlds in which they are true). Let X and Y be worlds: in our diagram they belong respectively to contrary propositions F(1) and F(2) in F-discourse. But in Q-discourse, both make Q(1) true. Hence things are different in X and in Y with respect to aspects expressible in F-sentences, but the same in any respect describable in Q-sentences. Therefore the F-discourse does not supervene on Q-discourse.

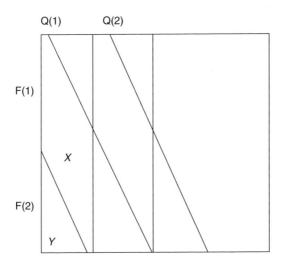

Conversely then, if one discourse does supervene on the other, we must be able to construe its propositions as such 'disjunctions'. This will not amount to reduction if these 'disjunctions' – which are sets whose elements are maximally consistent sets of sentences

– are not finite, not recursively enumerable, and not definable or specifiable in any other way.[29]

See how close this is to straightforward reduction! To have supervenience without reduction means to have no translation sentence by sentence or paragraph by paragraph or even definable set by definable set. . . . but there is still a perfect description 'at the far edge of infinity'.[30] The supervenience claim then still entails only that there is, so to speak, a reduction for God or for the angels, just not for finite beings like us.

This is obviously a position designed to be irrefutable. What are the benefits of believing in such a relation of persons to physical objects? The mere assurance of consistency? Cold comfort! Add to this that no such ideal 'physicalist' language exists, or is likely ever to be had . . . Why play these games?

'How does consciousness emerge?'

Once upon a time there were only inanimate objects; now there are living, behaving organisms, and some are conscious. How did consciousness emerge?

As a question for science, this is well-posed to the extent that the term 'consciousness' is well defined. But taken in that way, there is no problem in principle at all, regardless of one's philosophical stance. Agilulf's case can illustrate this point. At first sight his existence would raise the scientific problem: how could he possibly lift his sword? If there were such a knight, science would have the task of constructing an adequate model of the phenomena thus displayed. To begin it would produce a barely adequate model with little or no predictive power. That model would be replaced by a better one, and so on, as long as we had more factual questions to be answered and nature cooperated. The models would be accompanied by testable explanatory narratives.

What argument could there possibly be that scientists could not succeed in this? There are observable phenomena as the suit of

---

[29] Our specifications will be finite sets of sentences in our own language, of which there are only denumerably many, while even the family of 'state-descriptions' is already larger than that.

[30] I use Pascal's phrase, so apt in a similar context.

armor, sword, and shield move through the world; science models those phenomena. Whatever the phenomena are there can be a scientific story that depicts them, with unobservable things postulated and inserted if needed. That is simply what science does.

Similarly, there must necessarily be a scientific story about the transition classified as the emergence of consciousness. That is the change from when the world held as yet no living organisms to when it did, and from the states in which there was as yet no consciousness to when there was. The question 'how does consciousness emerge?' has therefore a very straightforward answer at any given time. That answer is provided by the model (perhaps still very unsatisfactory or inadequate) which science so far provides for that geological/biological stage. So we have an answer already, though it is as yet disappointingly uninformative; but it is improving all the time.

You can readily see the analogy between the relation of science to the emergence of consciousness (however defined) and Hume's confusion about miracles. Take any given miracle, such as water turning into wine. If this really happens, then physical science is adequate only if it implies the possibility of that happening. If scientists accepted it as a phenomenon to be accounted for, they would account for it. They would produce models, accompanied by explanatory stories, that fit the phenomenon. If the problem posed by the phenomenon is severe (as it was with radioactivity, for example) it may engender pervasive foundational changes in the natural sciences. The question 'How can miracles happen?' *cannot be* 'How can there be observable exceptions to empirically adequate scientific theories?' For the latter is self-contradictory.

Philosophers who confess themselves perplexed by the question *How could consciousness possibly have emerged at all in this physical world?* must be understanding the question in a different way, a way that has nothing to do with science. Their problem is a pseudo-problem unless (a) they have a clear and distinct understanding of this as different from the scientific question, and (b) they do not confuse the question so understood with the question as posed in any scientific context. I see no evidence that these desiderata are met.

There is a mystery of consciousness. But it is not among the mysteries that the sciences confront, which they so fortunately and habitually address and solve.

Disquisitions on substance

Does my account of the self not make it a substance?[31] The technical philosophical meaning departs, as usual, from our ordinary use, where cloth, water, and molasses are substances to be found in the home. One thing the technical question can mean is whether the self is a substance in the sense of 'a being which can subsist by itself, without dependence upon any other created being'. There is a rival technical construal perhaps equally familiar: 'the bearer of attributes, the subject of predication but is not itself predicable, that which receives modifications and is not itself a mode'. And there is a third, the most important one according to Leibniz: 'that which acts'.

Am I – is my self – a bearer of properties and a terminus of relations? Certainly, in the innocuous sense implied by the fact that I am thinking now, have a body subject to sickness, old age, and death, and have a brother as well as a disillusioned distant admirer perhaps, or something of the sort. Am I the subject of predication and not myself predicable? I should hope so. Do I act? There is no doubt that I do. Not only do I raise my arm, and respond to critical questions, but I do so deliberately and intentionally, thus clearly engaged in action and not just behavior.

Since my affirmative answers derive from very ordinary every–day assertions, for which I deny any need of metaphysical underpinning, I may still be misunderstanding the question. In any case, I have as yet omitted what is perhaps the most important sense. Am I – is the self – something that can subsist by itself, without dependence upon any other created being? Of course not. Suppose even (however implausibly) that for each person and thing in the world it is the case that I could have existed without it. It still does not follow that I could have existed without anything else at all.

If substances are things, then I am not a substance. If being a substance requires only that most ordinary things to be said about me are true, then I am. But of what use is that to metaphysical theorizing?

---

[31] Question very reasonably raised by Peter van Inwagen at the Reading conference.

CHAPTER 6

THE SELF: THE INCREDULOUS STARE ARTICULATED

Peter van Inwagen

This paper is an attempt to put into some sort of rational order some thoughts I have had about the self.[1] I confess that I haven't read much of what philosophers have said about the self.[2] But I've heard a fair number of philosophers talk about the self – Patricia Churchland, Daniel Dennett, Owen Flanagan – and I had the same reaction on each occasion: I did not understand what was being said. Galen Strawson's work on the self gets a different reaction from me: not the furrowed brow but the incredulous stare. At any rate, the incredulous stare is the reaction his theory would get from me if I did not sternly suppress it. Let me explain. It was of course David Lewis who enriched the technical vocabulary of the phenomenology of the reception of philosophical theories by the addition of the useful phrase 'the incredulous stare'. For quite a long while, although I understood the theory of possible worlds that Lewis said he accepted, I couldn't quite bring myself to believe that he really did believe what he said he believed about possible worlds. And I understand Galen's theory of the self, of multiple selves, of SESMENTS (Subjects of Experience that are Single MEntal Things) – or I think I do, although I have to make an effort to believe that he believes what he says he believes about selves. But I am determined to make the effort, for I have learned my lesson. I wasted a considerable amount of time *c.* 1980 trying to figure out what Lewis really believed about possible worlds, and I have since resolved to believe philosophers when they say they believe something.

---

[1]   I have revised this paper since it was presented at the conference whose proceedings are printed in this number of *Ratio*, but I have not tried to turn it into an essay. The reader will note that it represents itself as the text of a lecture – a lecture written to be delivered on a particular occasion, and to an audience that contained Galen Strawson.

[2]   With the exception of Galen Strawson. My understanding of his theory of the self is based on my reading of his essays 'The Self' [in R. Martin and J. Barresi, *Personal Identity* (Oxford: Blackwell, 2003), pp. 335–381; 'The Self' was first published in the *Journal of Consciousness Studies*, 4 (1997)] and 'The Self and SESMENTS,' *Journal of Consciousness Studies*, 6 (1999), pp. 99–135. Page references in square brackets in the text refer to the latter essay.

I will do two things. First, I'll set out Galen's theory as I understand it, or set out a part of it as I understand it. Secondly, I'll
explain why I find the theory so hard to believe – even as I resist
the temptation to find it hard to believe that Galen believes it.
Lewis, we remember, pointed out that an incredulous stare isn't
an argument. I have promised to refrain from directing any
incredulous stares at Galen (I've allowed the phrase to remain in
my title; one isn't obliged to be on one's best behavior in a title),
but, if an incredulous stare directed at the advocate of a theory
isn't an argument for the falsity of that theory, neither is the bare
statement that one finds that theory very hard to believe. Nevertheless, a careful attempt to articulate one's reasons for finding a
theory hard to believe can yield something like an argument for
the falsity of that theory. At any rate, making a careful attempt to
articulate my reasons for finding Galen's theory hard to believe
is the best I can do by way of an argument for its falsity. Indeed,
it's the best I can do by way of saying anything about it that could
conceivably be of philosophical interest to anyone.

Most philosophers who talk about the self face a simple
dilemma. Either one's self is what one refers to when one says 'I'
or it is not. If it is not – well, if something isn't oneself, why should
one call it one's self? If it is, then the thesis that there are no selves
entails that one does not exist; and the thesis that there are selves
is simply the thesis that one exists and (no doubt) that others like
one exist.[3]

This dilemma is obvious enough. That is, whether or not
there's a way for philosophers who talk of 'the self' (those who
affirm its existence and those who denounce it as a myth) to
escape from it, it's obvious enough that those philosophers ought
to have considered it and have something to say in response to it.
But none of the philosophers I have heard talk about the self
seems to have thought about it – or to have thought *of* it. When
I have tried to get them to think about it, various conversational
misfires follow, misfires of a kind I am familiar with from discussions of a wide range of philosophical questions. (It may be that
when, as I shall, I try to explain to Galen some of my reservations
about what he says about objects and processes, one of these misfires will occur.) When I try to explain to these philosophers what

---

[3]   For a more detailed presentation of this dilemma, see the first few pages of my essay,
'What Do We Refer to When We Say "I"?' in *The Blackwell Guide to Metaphysics*, Richard M.
Gale (ed.), Oxford: Basil Blackwell, 2002) pp. 175–189.

my problem about their use of the phrase 'the self' is, they very resolutely don't see what my problem with their use of the phrase is, and I don't see what their problem is with seeing what my problem is.

If, however, I were to confront *Galen* with my dilemma, there would be no room for a conversational misfire of the kind I have alluded to, for he is aware of the dilemma and has a response to it. He would tell me that it was a false dilemma because the word 'I' is ambiguous. When I use the word, or when the word issues from this mouth you see before you (he would tell me), the word refers in one of its senses to a person who has existed for many years, and in the other to that person's self, or, more precisely, to that person's *current* self. This is the *semantical* component of Galen's theory of the self. But the body of his theory is its metaphysical component: a series of connected theses about the nature of selves and the nature of persons, and the ways in which selves and persons are related. (The theory also has a phenomenological component, which I will not discuss.)

It is the metaphysical component of the theory I want to talk about. I am a person. (At any rate, he who reads this paper to you, reads the whole paper from beginning to end, is a person. In the sequel, I will ask you to take the words 'I' and 'me' and 'my' always to refer to the person before you and not to that person's current self. If you will grant this request, you will enable me to avoid a lot of annoying, repetitious parenthetical circumlocution. I promise that I will not abuse your indulgence; it is not my intention to undermine Galen's thesis that 'I' can refer either to the person who utters it or to the current self of that person by stipulating that *in this paper* it shall refer only to the person; I'm simply explicitly restricting the referent of 'I' *et al.* to one of things Galen says they refer to in order to simplify the syntax of what I'm going to say.) I am, I say, a person. I have constituent selves. What are these selves and what is their relation to me? Selves or SESMENTS are, Galen says, physical objects, just as persons are. (Galen is a materialist or physicalist. In this paper, I will take the truth of physicalism as given.)

SESMENTS are physical objects. They are, Galen says, peculiarly shaped things [131]. And *my* SESMENTS are parts of me. They compose me temporally as pearls compose a string of pearls spatially. I am a temporal sequence of SESMENTS. (Does this mean that SESMENTS are temporal parts of me? I'll try to talk round this question, to make no explicit commitments as regards the ontology of diachronic composition.) Each of my SESMENTs is a subject of experience, as I am, but one with a much briefer temporal span than mine, perhaps only a second or two. Each SESMENT, moreover, has a particular kind of unity that makes it a real physical object and not an arbitrary non-unity like the mereological sum of the Thames, Nikita Khrushchev's head, and the bottom half of the Empire State Building. And this is the point at which the semantical component of the theory joins the metaphysical. 'I' is like 'now' and 'the world' in that it can, so to speak, refer to more or to less. When I say, 'Everybody push when I say 'now' – one, two, three, *now!*', the word 'now' refers to 'less'; when a surly teenager says, 'That was then, this is now,' the word refers to 'more.' But, if the two utterances are simultaneous, 'less' is a part of 'more.' Or consider the phrase 'the world', which may refer to the inhabited parts of the surface of the earth, to the entire surface of the earth, to the planet (the whole solid ball), and to the cosmos. That is to say, 'the world' may refer, depending on context, to less or to more, and 'less' must be a proper part of 'more.' The word 'I' is, as I have said, like 'now' and 'the world'. On a particular occasion of utterance, it may refer either to a person (a long-lasting subject of experience) or to that person's current self (a short-lived subject of experience). The latter case is the case of 'less,' the former case the case of 'more.' And 'less,' is a proper part of 'more,' for one's current self is a part of one. Anyone who attempts to adapt the dilemma I have urged on various philosophers who speak of the self to Galen's theory and who contends that my current SESMENT (supposing there to be an object that has the right properties to count as my current SESMENT) cannot properly be called my current *self* because it is not I is mistaken, because my current SESMENT is one of the possible referents of my utterance of 'I'. The sentence 'I have existed for over sixty years' can express a truth and so can the sentence 'I have existed for only a second or so', just as the two sentences 'The world is eight thousand miles in diameter' and 'The world is billions of light-years in diameter' can both express truths.

There is a lot more to Galen's theory than this. (I have, for example, said nothing about the features of a SESMENT that make it a non-arbitrary unity. A discussion of these features would require an exposition of the phenomenological component of his theory. It will suffice for my purposes simply to note that, according to the theory, there *are* features of SESMENTs in virtue of which they have a non-arbitrary kind of unity.) But this is enough for me to go on with. I can now explain why I find the theory so hard to believe, no matter what other constituent theses it might have. I am a person (the theory says), and I have constituent selves. Certain parts of me are peculiarly shaped physical objects called selves. Right now a current part of me, a currently existing physical object, is my current self. And these things are *real* things, not some sort of useful fiction, as, perhaps, shadows or waves or holes or wrinkles are. But I have questions. I think they are good questions, but that doesn't mean that I think Galen can't answer them. In fact, I think I know what his answers would be. Nonetheless, it will be useful to ask the questions and listen to his answers.

If selves or SESMENTs are real things, then the following is true of each of them: for every property, it has either that property or its complement. And what *are* the properties of SESMENTs? Well, consider my current self. It's a physical thing, we're told, a peculiarly shaped physical thing that's a part of me. But then *what* is its peculiar shape? And how big is it? What region of space does it occupy? What is its mass? How many atoms is it composed of? If it's a physical thing, surely, it must have (in addition to a shape) a size and a mass? It must (must it not?) occupy a certain region of space, for how could a thing have a shape and not occupy some region of space? But then why aren't these SESMENTs known to anatomists, albeit under some other name? I don't expect that a forensic pathologist examining a murder victim would say anything like, 'The man's self seems to be relatively intact', but one would expect that if SESMENTs were real physical parts of us, anatomists would know about SESMENTs even if they didn't know they were selves. (Unless, perhaps, they were very small, and for that reason didn't show up even in CAT scans or PET scans.)

Here is what I take Galen's answer to this question to be. (The words that follow are mine, not his.)

You must overcome your subservience to the object-process dichotomy. Consider a performance of, say, 'Pictures at an Exhibition' – by a particular pianist on a particular occasion. This is a physical object. It's a peculiarly shaped one in that it occupies a peculiarly shaped region of space-time. But it's no argument against the reality of this object that we can't say what its mass is, or could only by making some extremely artificial stipulation. SESMENTs are in certain respects like performances of musical works. There are questions one could sensibly ask about someone's pineal gland or a grand piano ('How much does it weigh?', for example) such that, if one can't sensibly ask those same questions about a self or a per-

formance, it doesn't follow that selves or performances aren't physical objects in the same sense as that in which pineal glands or grand pianos are physical objects.

But I see you stirring in protest. I bet I know what you're going to say. You're going to tell me that a musical performance is not, as I have said it is, an object but an event or process. And you're going to tell me that you strongly suspect that a SESMENT is likewise an event or process and that my theory must therefore entail that a self is an event or process. You will tell me, finally, that a self, whatever else it may be, must be an object, not an event. A self, you will argue, is supposed to be a part of a person, and although many brief events are parts of the long event that is a person's life, no event can be a part of an object or continuant or substance – and a person is an object. A self, moreover, is supposed to be a subject of experience, and an event can't be a subject of experience: an experience is an event, but the subject of an experience can't be an event. I have anticipated your protest. Recall the words with which I began: You must overcome your subservience to the object-process dichotomy. [Note in propria persona: Although I have written the speech I'm putting into Galen's mouth, several of its key sentences are direct quotations from 'The Self and the SESMENTs.'] There is no sense in which a SESMENT is a process in which a rock is not also and equally a process. [125] It's wrong to think that if a physical process occurs there must be physical objects that, for the duration of the process, collectively occupy the region of space in which the process takes place, and which are such that the changes in the intrinsic properties of those objects, and the changes in the relations they bear to one another, constitute that process. This may be true according to our pre-theoretical conception of objects and processes, but we know that the world frequently refuses to behave in the ways our pre-theoretical conceptions lead us to expect. There is no ontologically weighty distinction between an object and a process. [126] There is no defensible concept of an object – a spatio-temporal continuant, as philosophers say – that allows one to distinguish validly between objects and processes by saying that one is an essentially dynamic or changeful phenomenon and the other is not [126].

So speaks Galen, at least in my imagination. I wish to make three points in reply.

First, what he says is very heavy on assertion and very light on argument. It's no worse for that, but the fact should be recognized. Secondly, there is an important argument he does not address. I think that an adequate solution to the problem that this argument presents is possible within the constraints of his theory, but the point is worth raising. The argument is based on an example of Davidson's. Consider a ball that is both rotating and heating up. The rotation of the ball and the warming of the ball are distinct events or processes. But if there is no distinction to be made between an object and an event, then, it would seem, each must be identical with the ball, and hence with the other. Here is what I would say about this problem if I were, like Galen, an advocate of the deconstruction of the object-process dichotomy. The ball is (is not to be distinguished from) the sum of all the processes taking place in the ball-shaped region of space it occupies. This sum is itself a process, or as good a candidate for the dubious office 'process' as anything is. The rotation of the ball and the warming of the ball are two distinct proper parts of this total process, rather as 'orbiting the earth' and 'orbiting the sun' are two distinct components of the moon's corkscrew trajectory. The ball, the total process, the rotation, and the warming are all physical objects and physical objects in the same sense (three physical objects, not four, since 'the ball' and 'the total process' are two names for the same physical object).

Thirdly and finally, I want to say something about the following sentence of Galen's (it is one of the direct quotations that were included in the speech that, for the most part, I wrote for him):

> There is no defensible concept of an object – a spatio-temporal continuant, as philosophers say – that allows one to distinguish validly between objects and processes by saying that one is an essentially dynamic or changeful phenomenon and the other is not.

I don't think anyone has ever thought that physical objects are not essentially dynamic and changeful, otherwise than because that person thought, like the Eleatics and McTaggart, that *nothing* was dynamic and changeful. That is, I don't think anyone has thought that physical objects were not dynamic and changeful and that something else *was*. How could that be? Physical objects, or most of them, change their intrinsic properties with the passage of time, and (if change exists at all) what could be more dynamic and changeful than that? What could being dynamic and changeful be *but* that? Or is the idea that objects could in principle be 'frozen' and remain objects, while a frozen process would not be an process at all? If so, I would say that if this observation is supposed to show that there is something wrong with the object-

process distinction, it is unconvincing because it depends crucially on a verbal accident. Objects and processes and the distinction between them can be believed in and objects and
processes can nevertheless be regarded as perfectly parallel with
respect to change and unchange (if that is what one wants) by a
simple verbal adjustment. Simply do what some philosophers have
done for reasons unrelated to Galen's point: regard 'unchanges'
as perfectly good, if rather special, kinds of events or processes –
just as, in kinematics, 0 cm/sec is a perfectly good, if rather
special, velocity. On that understanding of 'process', processes,
like objects, do not essentially involve change; and it seems to be
a mere accident that we have not adopted that understanding of
'process.'

But these three points are minor points. A general metaphysical framework cannot be refuted, or to the least degree rendered
implausible, by the presentation of minor points. And we must
consider the general metaphysical framework in which Galen
embeds his ontology of the self if we wish to evaluate that theory,
for the theory is indefensible except in the terms provided by the
general metaphysical framework. Selves must be processes, brief
episodes in a person's mental life, if their temporal span is to be as
brief as Galen says it is. And selves must be possible referents of
the word 'I' if they are really to be selves. And any referent of 'I'
must be an object. These requirements are inconsistent if 'object'
and 'process' are distinct and incompatible ontological categories. And, therefore, Galen's theory is defensible only if 'object'
and 'process' are *not* distinct and incompatible ontological
categories.

I must say that I have a very hard time understanding Galen's
larger metaphysical framework. (The 'larger metaphysical framework' is not, as I see it, a part of the theory of SESMENTs, although
it figures in, and is in fact essential to, Galen's defence of the
theory against an important objection. The statement I have just
made is therefore consistent with my earlier claim to understand
the theory of SESMENTs.) One aspect, at least, of the framework,
its refusal to countenance the 'object-process dichotomy', simply
bewilders me. If I may borrow these well-known words, let me see
whether I can say something to evoke the appropriate sense of
bewilderment – or at any rate, say something that will explain my
own bewilderment. I will try to do this by laying out a metaphysical framework of my own, the general system of categories that I
use to think about things.

Are you sitting comfortably? Then I'll begin. The most general metaphysical category is the category 'thing.' I use 'thing' as the most general count-noun. Everything is a thing. A thing is anything that can be referred to by a third-person-singular pronoun – as when I say, 'The following is true of everything, that it is identical with itself.' The category 'thing' comprises everything there is, everything that exists (for I take a stern anti-Meinongian line about non-existents: non-existents simply don't exist: the number of them is 0).

Things divide into two subcategories, the concrete and the abstract. If there are such things as the following, they are concrete: cabbages, kings, bits of sealing wax, electrons, tables and chairs, angels, pixies, and God. I myself believe in only some of the things in this list: cabbages, kings, electrons, angels, and God.[4] But I am quite certain that if there *were* bits of sealing wax, tables and chairs, and pixies, they *would be* concrete things. Here is a list of abstract things: propositions, possibilities, sentence-types, sets, properties or attributes, numbers, novels (as opposed to tangible copies of novels), theories, and such miscellaneous items as the key of F-sharp minor, democracy, and the literary form *the epic poem*. I am not sure which of the things in this list I believe really exist (I certainly think some of them do), but I am quite certain that if there is such a thing as, for example, the key of F-sharp minor, it is an abstract thing.

There is only one kind of concrete thing: that which has traditionally been called 'substance' or 'individual thing'. (This is what corresponds in my framework to Galen's category 'object'.) And there is only one type of abstract thing. I will call this one type 'relation.' I will first expand on this statement. Among relations there are 0-term relations, or propositions, 1-term relations (also called properties, attributes, qualities, features, characteristics, . . .), and 2-or-more-term relations, which I will call 'proper relations' (on the model of proper fractions and proper subsets). I will not discuss proper relations. I will, however, say something about propositions and properties. Propositions are things that have truth-values. They are things that can be *said*; that is, asserted. They are things that can be assented to or denied. (For most propositions, these descriptions are true only in principle,

---

[4]   For my reasons for thinking that there are no bits of sealing wax and no tables and chairs, see my book *Material Beings* (Ithaca: Cornell University Press, 1990). My reasons for thinking that there are no pixies are more straightforward.

at least as regards human beings.) Properties, by contrast, are things that can be *said of* or *about* something (whether truly or falsely); that it is white, for example. That it is white is one of the things you can say truly about the White House, and you can say it truly about the Taj Mahal, too. But you can't say it truly of the Eiffel Tower or the key of F-sharp minor; you can, in fact, say it only falsely of these things, for (if there indeed are such things as these) each is non-white. A few properties have traditional names that are, as the linguists say, perfect nominals: 'whiteness', for example, or 'wisdom'. In my view, 'wisdom' is a name for what we say *of* or *about* Solomon and the Cumaean Sibyl when, speaking with reference to them, we say, as appropriate, 'He is wise' or 'She is wise'. But most properties have no such names: one of the things we can say of something is that it is one of the two daughters of the forty-third President of the U.S. (we could say this truly of exactly two things; if we said it of Chelsea Clinton or the Eiffel Tower or the number of planets, we'd be saying it falsely of those things). And this property, a perfectly good example of a property in my view, has no one-word name. Typical properties (and, more generally, typical relations) are, as 'whiteness' and 'wisdom' and our more complicated example testify, universals, for, typically, a property can be said truly of – or, to use some more usual idioms, can belong to, be had by, be instantiated by, be exemplified by – two or more things. Not all properties have this feature, however, for there are plenty of things that can be said truly of only one thing (that it is a daughter of the forty-second president; that it is an even prime), and plenty that cannot be said truly of even one thing (that it is a woman who served as President of the U.S. in the twentieth century; that it is both round and square). I thus come down on the side of Platonism, as opposed both to nominalism and Aristotelianism. And a very capacious Platonism it is. I'd *like* to say that to every meaningful open sentence there corresponds a property, but Russell's paradox stands in my way.[5]

I should at some point mention that Galen attempts to deconstruct not only the object-process distinction, but the object-property distinction as well. I didn't mention the object-property distinction earlier because its relevance to the philosophy of the

---

[5] For some remarks on Russell's Paradox and on many other issues raised by the theory of properties of which I have presented a brief sketch in the text, see my essay 'A Theory of Properties,' *Oxford Studies in Metaphysics*, Vol. 1, Dean Zimmerman (ed.), (Oxford: Oxford University Press, 2004) pp. 107–138.

self is less clear to me than is the relevance of the object-process distinction. I mention it now because the object-property distinction (or, in my terms, the substance-property distinction) is crucial to my metaphysical framework. I must also mention the fact that Galen and I do not seem to be talking about the same sort of thing when we use the word 'property'. He would say that what I am calling properties are universals and that what he calls properties are what should, strictly speaking, be called property-*instances*. One often encounters this term in discussions of the metaphysics of properties, but I have never been able to understand it. It would seem to me that an instance of the property whiteness would not itself be a property in any possible sense of the word but rather a white thing – the Taj Mahal, for example. (If Galen were to reply to this objection, I am pretty sure that one of those conversational misfires would ensue.) In connection with his rejection of the object-property distinction, Galen more than once quotes the following sentence from the *Critique of Pure Reason*: '. . . in their relation to substance, accidents [Galen equates Kant's "accidents" and his own property-instances] are not really subordinated to it, but are the mode of existing of the substance itself'. The only response I can make to this sentence is the furrowed brow I mentioned earlier. In any case, *my* properties, universals, are certainly distinct from substances. What could be more clearly a proper distinction than the distinction between Socrates and the things one can say truly about Socrates?

If I had not explicitly classified them as such, it would be evident from what I have said about them that (what I call) properties are abstract objects. And abstract objects cannot be 'constituents' of substances. (Whatever that might mean. So far as I can see, the only constituents of a material substance like a chair are smaller material substances, such as legs and screws and cellulose molecules.) If there are such things as 'tropes' ('trope', I suppose, is another word for 'property-instance') or 'immanent universals,' they are not properties or any other sort of relation. And, since, in my view, there are only substances and relations, there are no tropes or immanent universals. I don't mind this consequence, for, as far as I can see, the term 'trope' (as used by philosophers), and the term 'immanent universal' are perfectly meaningless. Another perfectly meaningless term – this one over on the 'concrete' side of things – would be 'bare particular'. (Here, finally, is a point in which Galen and I are in complete agreement.) A bare particular would either be what you get when you subtract the tropes from an ordinary substance (and thus the term would be meaningless) or else a thing of which nothing is true; and, of course, the idea of a thing of which nothing is true makes no sense at all.

Now I must try to say something useful about substances or individual things. I can think of only two useful things to say. First, following Aristotle, I can say that a substance is a thing that has properties but is not itself a property. (Since I think that the only concrete things are substances, might I not define a concrete thing as a thing that has properties but is not itself a property? I will not, for I think that I have an independent grasp of the concepts *concrete thing* and *substance*, and I mean my thesis that the only concrete things are substances to be a substantive metaphysical thesis.) Secondly, it follows from what I have said that substances have causal powers and that anything that has causal powers is a substance. (For concrete things and only concrete things have causal powers, and I have said that the only concrete things are substances.) Some philosophers will be unhappy with this feature of my metaphysical framework. Perhaps you are one of them. Perhaps you think that there are things that have causal powers but are not substances. If you do, I'll have to ask you what those things might be. Tropes? There are no such things. Surfaces? There are no such things. States? *Either* there are no such things or they are some sort of property and thus lack causal powers. Social entities like football teams and corporations? I don't know what to say about them, other than to remind you that hard cases make bad law. (I don't mean that I can't think of any way to fit social entities into my ontological framework; I mean I can think of lots of ways to fit them in, and am not sure which is the best.)

Stuffs? Well, stuffs are worthy of discussion, but it seems to me that one of the lessons of science is that 'stuff' cannot function as a fundamental category for understanding the world. For a region of space to be filled with butter or tin is, we now know, for that region to contain elementary particles arranged in certain specific ways. And elementary particles are not made of stuffs.

Events? Ah, that's a very good question, and very much to the present point. In my view, there are no events. True statements that apparently imply the existence of events can, I contend, be paraphrased as statements solely about the changing properties of and changing relations among substances. This is the feature of my metaphysical framework at which it is most obviously in conflict with Galen's metaphysical framework. Galen maintains that there are objects (which are more or less what I call substances) and processes (it is evident that 'process' and 'event' must either be the same category or else that 'process' must be a sub-category of 'event'), but that objects and processes are, to put the matter crudely, the *same thing*: the supposed *distinction* between them is, at the level of fundamental ontology, an illusion. I maintain that 'substance' is a fundamental ontological category and that there are no events. True, substances change their properties, and the relations among them change. At one time I am cold and ten feet from Galen; at another I am warm and hundreds of miles from him. But it does not follow from the fact that things change that there are such things as changes. Or, contraposing, from the premise that there are no such things as changes, the conclusion does not follow that things do not change.

One who accepts my metaphysical framework must therefore say that if there are selves they are substances. And substances are in no sense events or processes. Substances are in no sense processes for two reasons. First, as I have said, there are no processes for them to be. Secondly, if there *were* processes, they would have the wrong properties for them to be substances – just as, if there were pixies, they would have the wrong properties to be elephants. Events or processes, if they existed, would begin, end, happen, take place, go on, or occur. They would be changes in the intrinsic properties of or the relations among substances. Substances come into being and pass away; they last or endure or get older; if they are material substances, they have masses. And these properties are not properties events would have if they existed. I do not see a place for selves, as distinct from persons, in a world whose fundamental ontology is the way I believe the fundamental ontology of the actual world (and, indeed, of any possible world) to be. If Galen is right, then every time I complete a certain unified episode of thought-and-feeling, a self ends; one pearl in the string that composes me, the person, is over. But I am convinced that, on such occasions, no substance ceases to exist.

This is, of course, no argument against the existence of selves or SESMENTS. It is no argument against the existence of *xs* to point out that there is no place for *xs* in the general metaphysical framework one favors. But I haven't introduced my metaphysical framework with a view to presenting an argument against the existence of selves. I didn't arrive at my general picture of the world in order to have a picture of the world that has no place for selves. But, in the end, I *do* have a picture of the world that has, or seems to have, no place in it for selves. It seems that, at any rate as regards Galen and me, the debate about the existence of selves must be set aside and replaced by a debate about existence-in-general, about which general metaphysical framework to accept.

INDEX